TRUE CONFESSIONS

from the Ninth Concession

DAN NEEDLES

Douglas & McIntyre

Douglas and McIntyre (2013) Ltd.
P.O. Box 219, Madeira Park, BC, V0N 2H0
www.douglas-mcintyre.com

Cover illustration by Wesley W. Bates
Cover design by Anna Comfort O'Keeffe
Text design by Mary White
Photo opposite the Introduction is from the author's collection
Thinkstock illustrations by: asmakar (pages 59, 65, 119, 133, 167); geraria (pages 11, 20); la_puma (pages 35, 68, 88, 103, 131, 141, 162, 173, 199, 200, 217); mubai (pages 47, 208); Val_Iva (pages 15, 205). Other illustrations by T. Karbashewski (pages 27, 150, 190, 211).
Printed on FSC-certified paper made with 100% post-consumer waste
Printed and bound in Canada

Douglas and McIntyre (2013) Ltd. acknowledges the support of the Canada Council for the Arts, which last year invested $153 million to bring the arts to Canadians throughout the country. We also gratefully acknowledge financial support from the Government of Canada through the Canada Book Fund and from the Province of British Columbia through the BC Arts Council and the Book Publishing Tax Credit.

Library and Archives Canada Cataloguing in Publication

Needles, Dan, author
    True confessions from the ninth concession / Dan Needles.

Issued in print and electronic formats.
ISBN 978-1-77162-169-4 (softcover).--ISBN 978-1-77162-170-0 (HTML)

    1. Needles, Dan. 2. Farmers--Ontario--Humor. 3. Farm life--Ontario--Humor. 4. Farms, Small--Ontario--Humor. 5. Authors, Canadian (English)--20th century--Biography. I. Title.

PS8577.E333Z46 2017   C813'.54   C2017-902721-2
                                       C2017-902722-0

To my neighbour, Hughie
I'll see you after

It's hard to be a good neighbour and grow zucchini.
—Hugh McKee (1943–2016)

Table of Contents

This Old House

I first saw the little frame farmhouse in early spring 1978 when I was young and single and still working in the city. It looked like the last hideout of Jesse James and Cole Younger. It sat on the Ninth Concession of Old Nottawasaga Township, a dead-end road in the shadow of the Niagara Escarpment, with a view of Georgian Bay away to the north. The windows were broken and most of the rolled asphalt siding had shredded away in the wind, exposing the original pine boards. The stone foundation had crumbled beneath it, and two ancient barn beams had been stuck under it to prevent it from sinking into the rubble. A cow stood in the kitchen, gazing at me through the open door. I remember joking to the realtor, "This listing will not last."

Even then the house had a long history as a weekend property. The last owner to take a serious interest in the place was a local boy who moved to the city before the Second World War to work as a welder but returned faithfully for holidays and long weekends until his death in 1968. Then it passed through the usual indignities of a rundown country property: flipped, rented, pastured and generally vandalized. The lilac and spirea bushes on the bank overlooking the stream told me that it had once been loved, but now the house was a home for mice, raccoons . . . and a cow.

The house had a good feeling to it, and I kept finding little treasures that could be saved. The pine floors were four inches thick and the wood stove still worked. I salvaged a cast-iron floor lamp and turned the skylight above the front door into a hall mirror. In the front yard were four ancient Bartlett pear trees that produced fat yellow pears in August. My neighbour helped me locate the spiderweb of clay drainage tiles in the fields. Digging in the garden I found potsherds, pieces of French copper and stone tools left here by the Petun Indians of the seventeenth century.

That first summer a group of friends helped me stage a plaster-bashing weekend, and so began the slow process of weekend renovations on a tight budget. I built a new foundation farther back from the road, hired a crane to move the house and remodelled it inside and out. Every summer for the next ten years I took on some new project—tree planting, a veranda, stone walls, rail and page-wire fences—and gradually the property came back to life.

In 1977 there hadn't been a child born on the Blind Line, as it was called, since the 1940s. My three immediate neighbours were all bachelors like me. Then suddenly the curse broke and within ten years there were babies everywhere. Heath and I got married in 1987 and the following spring we both quit our jobs in the city and moved to the farm to start a family and my career as a writer. The moment she set foot in the house, Heath announced it had a good feel to it and was just waiting to be made into a home and loved. Our first daughter arrived that fall, and for three cozy winters we lived in a space that wasn't much bigger than our apartment in the city. We built a new sheep barn, more fences and a bigger garden, and started bringing hay in from the fields every summer. After our second child was born, we built an addition that doubled our living space. Two more children followed and a lot of animals.

Shortly after we moved here full-time the welder's widow, Nellie, came by on a Sunday outing from her nursing home, but we were away and missed her. She left a note in a shaky scrawl saying that she and her husband had always wanted to move back here and do what we had done with the farm and she wished us well. I was glad that her lilacs, spireas and pear trees hadn't been disturbed.

In 1997 Tom Cruickshank, the editor of *Harrowsmith Magazine*, called me up and asked if I would take over the back page that Timothy Findley had occupied for several years with his "Stone Orchard" column. Tom and I decided to call it "True Confessions from the Ninth Concession." The assignment lasted for fifteen years until the magazine folded in 2012. Then "True Confessions" moved to a trio of quarterly Ontario publications: *In The Hills* (Dufferin-Caledon), *On The Bay* (Georgian Bay) and *Watershed* (Cobourg-Port Hope), where it continues to this day.

These pieces tell the story of a family growing up in a farm neighbourhood that is undergoing rapid change. The old farms are joined to make vast cash-crop acreages, and the houses give up their bachelors in favour of young families like my own. The party telephone line gives way to the internet. In spite of all the new children, the local school closes. Teenagers decide it should be called the prison farm. They go away to school and work, and then they eventually return looking for something they haven't found in the city. They look at our little oasis, and I see them wondering how on earth they are supposed to find a place like this for themselves in the world today. I tell them that life is a constructed thing. You build it one little piece at a time. And eventually, if you're very lucky, you look back at a faded photo of yourself standing in a stiff breeze in front of an abandoned house in a treeless pasture and you shake your head wondering, "What on earth was I thinking?"

From Here to Maternity

M y wife and I decided to leave the city ten years ago when she was expecting our first child. Heath is a farm girl and, while I wasn't born on a farm, my childhood was divided between winters in the city and long idyllic summers on a rundown pasture farm sixty miles north of Toronto. We didn't want the baby's first home to be a high-rise, so we quit our jobs in the city, packed everything up and moved to a forty-acre farm south of Georgian Bay.

Heath loved the adventure of living in a downtown apartment in Toronto the first year we were married, but she was puzzled that our city friends displayed little interest in her pregnancy. They offered polite congratulations at dinner parties but nothing compared to the enthusiasms of her circle up here.

Heath's sisters, cousins, aunts, neighbours and friends take on a pregnancy as a community project. They set up quilting frames, knit industrial quantities of booties and socks, and pick out the baby's first firearm. The sisterhood is also a reliable source of suspect medical information. To determine whether the baby is a boy or a girl they examine the twist in the hair of the last baby born in the family. Sometimes they float a needle on a thread over the mother's tummy to confirm the findings of the hair test. They admit these tests are not foolproof but insist they are more reliable than ultrasound.

When the big day finally arrives, the sisterhood is very sensitive about the order in which they are informed of the birth. Mother comes first, sisters next in strict order of age, of course, and then on to other family favourites: best friend, closest neighbour, senior members of the fair board and the church auxiliary. None of this is necessary, because the nurses all went to school with the other sisters and have already called them from the hospital cafeteria. Everyone pretends to be surprised.

Last year, when one of Heath's friends had her first baby, I got to watch the Network in action. I took my car into the garage in town and listened to the following conversation over the snarl of impact air hammers:

"I think Maureen's water broke last night."

"Yeah, I called Eric late and there was no answer."

"And the car wasn't at the house this morning."

"I just did a lap of the hospital and his car wasn't in the parking lot."

"She must have gone toxic like her sister and they took her to the Regional."

Three mechanics came to the correct conclusion that Maureen was indeed in labour, but because of some complication had been taken to the regional hospital in Barrie . . . and these were all young bachelors working on exhaust pipes and listening to Aerosmith on Rock 95.

When we were expecting our fourth this spring, I learned that sometimes the Network fouls up because faulty information is unintentionally fed into the system by someone like me. On Heath's due date the sink backed up, and I discovered that the sewer line to our septic tank had collapsed. While I was digging out the line under the porch, I made the mistake of telling one of the neighbours on the phone that we had a water problem once again.

"What are you going to do about it?" she asked.

"I've got more important things to think about," I said.

When this news went around the Network, people were thoroughly alarmed that I hadn't taken Heath straight to the hospital, and a delegation met me on the veranda to intervene.

If you live anywhere between Highway 9 and Georgian Bay, you will have already heard the news that Heath was delivered of a bouncing baby girl named Hannah. Mother and child are doing fine, thank you.

Home Sweet Home Office

I've been working out of the house on our farm for ten years now and it still amazes me how little you have to do to stay competitive with people who work in conventional offices. After all, once you take the commuting, meetings and pointless business luncheons out of your day, you automatically gain a seven-hour advantage over everybody else.

Take last week, for example. I was facing a deadline for a magazine piece and had given myself the day to work on it. I rose early, fed the sheep and cows, milked my goat, drove the children to school at 8:30, had a cup of coffee with my wife and finally headed down the hall to my office. I sat down at the keyboard at 9:00 a.m. The day stretched out like a carpet before me. At 9:15 I was lowering myself into the writer's private world, which is a limbo somewhere between semi-consciousness and a proper nap, when my wife appeared in the doorway.

"I'm sorry to bother you, but the Walrus just had twins and I need you to set up a pen for her."

This is the sort of interruption you have to expect when you run a farm as a sideline to the home office. I rose and went to the barn, separated the old ewe from the rest of the flock, gave her a drink and a flake of hay and made sure the lambs were sucking.

Half an hour later I settled back at the keyboard and returned to my pastoral essay.

The phone rang. It was a lady from the school explaining that my son was acting out the life cycle of a mosquito in the school play tonight and he would need some eggs. I promised to bring some over when I picked up the kids. As I rang off I looked up and saw my three-year-old coming down the stairs triumphantly waving an open pill bottle. I cleared the baby gate with a single bound and snatched it up. He had found his older brother's supply of chewable fluoride tablets and was popping them like peppermint candies, which is pretty much what they taste like. We spent the next half-hour on the phone to the dentist, the doctor and the Poison Information Centre. They all assured us that he had not taken enough to constitute a toxic dose and would probably be fine if we just gave him a glass of milk. We did and he threw up.

"This isn't working for you," said my wife. "Why don't I take the kids down to my mum's and leave you in peace for the afternoon?"

Half an hour later she left and a dreadful calm descended over the house. I find that the wrong kind of noise, like dogfights and falling lamps, can be distracting. But total silence is even worse. I work best with a low level of routine household white noise: kids playing, dogs chewing furniture, reassuring kitchen noises. I went into the kitchen to make some of those noises. I was just padding back to my office with a toasted cheese sandwich when I looked out the window and saw a Jersey cow loping by on the road. My cow, of course. I jumped into my rubber boots and jogged out to the road to find that I was the last person in the neighbourhood to know that my cows were out. Susie McLeod was blocking them from reaching the sideroad with her Ford Explorer, waiting for reinforcements. Ken Ferguson had stopped his truck out at the corners and recruited Rose Marie Robinson from her orchard. Josh McKee had left his disc harrows and was trudging across the field in our direction.

By normal cow chasing standards it wasn't much of a breakout. The cows were just impatient to get out onto green pasture and had pushed their way past a loose doorpost to the freedom of the open road. When they found themselves surrounded, they surrendered peacefully and walked back into the barnyard without a struggle. I repaired the doorpost and strung electric fence around the barnyard. As I was walking back to the house, George Caughill skidded to a halt on the road and called to me that he'd just seen a fox carrying one of my chickens away from the henhouse.

When my wife drove in at 3:15, I was standing on the front lawn with a shovel.

"Have you finished that piece?" she asked.

"No," I shouted. "I've been chasing cows and foxes and repairing buildings and burying chickens and now I have to go buy some eggs because they're re-enacting the 1952 Encephalitis Scare at the school tonight. When am I supposed to get anything written around here!"

She led me back into the house to the keyboard and patted me on the shoulder.

"I'll get the eggs for the school play," she said. "You just sit here and write."

"What about?" I said glumly.

"Why don't you write about your day?" she suggested and gently closed the door.

The Pickle Factory

The cluster flies have come back to Nottawasaga Township, which is perhaps not so romantic an image as the return of the Capistrano swallows but still a very certain sign that summer is over. I sometimes wonder if the Egyptian pharaoh in the time of Moses might have cracked sooner if the Lord had sent cluster flies instead of frogs and locusts. Each year at this time they return in their millions and turn the west walls of every building black. In the loft of the barn where the heat is greatest, the roar of their wings is louder than rain on the roof. They come home to die, of course, forming thick carpets on the floor of any house that isn't hermetically sealed.

In these dry, still days when the sedge has withered from the lake and no birds sing, it's hard to remember that in just a few months the mercury will shrivel to a dot at the bottom of the thermometer and the land will turn to stone. I look at the roadside thick with sweet clover and try to imagine snow squeaking underfoot, smoke from the chimney rising straight up for a hundred feet and all the residents of the Ninth Concession dug in and snug like prairie chickens.

It is not a feat of imagining for my wife, who is from a fifth-generation farm family. As soon as the first cluster fly arrives, she is already well into her preparations for nuclear winter. I've explained to her that food is still available in supermarkets even after the first frost, but there's a part of her that doesn't really believe it. She and her mother run a full-time cannery and pickle factory from the middle of August on, and they don't stop until they have filled four freezers and forty feet of basement shelves with every fruit and vegetable that can be put through a blender or a juicer. They visit secret groves of elderberries and like nine-year-olds clamber along rail fences in search of black caps (raspberries). They make brandied peaches using bottles of plonk that Italian hunters have presented to us in return for an afternoon's shooting. Two years ago the two of them found an abandoned grove of highbush cran-berries and spent an afternoon concocting a brew that became known in our house as "wet dog jelly."

I do my part through all of this, stuffing the barn full of hay and grain and adding to the stockpile of firewood. When I get a moment to sit on the veranda and catch my breath, I see lines of camper vans on the highway in the distance, a reminder that this is supposed to be vacation season. But in the culture of this town-ship, a man's role in September is to put away machinery, plug holes on the windward side of buildings and find firewood.

It's ridiculous, I suppose. Something really should be done about these archaic rituals, beginning with this business of the wood. After a decade of wrestling with chainsaws, pickup

trucks, hay wagons and wood splitters, I have found that the most sensible and cheapest way to heat the house is to move the thermostat gently to the right with my index finger and go read a book. As far as the machinery goes, I know summer is over when the lawn tractor finally returns from the small engine dealership, where it has rested for most of the season, waiting for parts. It arrives back just in time to be put away for the winter.

There are probably cheaper and more useful ways to occupy ourselves but, just as my wife enjoys ladling out ninety-proof helpings of peaches to her friends in front of the wood stove on a crackling cold December evening, I like to stand under the stars in the barnyard and smell the sweetness of a steamy cow chomping on green hay and crushed corn. At moments like these, utility and profit are far from our minds, which is as it should be.

Making Our Own Fun

Three years ago the minister of our little church asked me to write a Christmas play that could be performed by a group of actors selected from the congregations of the three tiny churches in her rural parish.

I wrote a little story about a man named Ralph who retires to the village of Duntroon and has difficulty fitting into the rhythms of country life. He finds the neighbours standoffish, and his one attempt to make a community contribution is politely but firmly rejected. A long walk, a blizzard, a series of visions and a lost cow combine to bring him to a closer understanding of his neighbours and his adopted community.

The minister assigned parts to twenty-one people and found me a stage manager, a lighting director, a wardrobe mistress, a sound technician and a pianist. We borrowed a set of risers for a stage and theatre lights from the high school, painted a beautiful cow's head and invented a brilliant snowstorm with piles of shredded tissue paper and a fan.

The rehearsal schedule was chaotic. People were so busy in the weeks leading up to the play that we never actually had a single run-through with everyone present. The night before we opened, my wife and I went to bed shaking our heads and wondering why on earth we had ever taken this project on.

But everyone turned up on time the next evening. The lights dimmed in the parish hall, and Ralph's odyssey began under the critical gaze of a large crowd of neighbours from the Parish of Duntroon, Singhampton and Batteaux. The audience started to chuckle during Ralph's encounter with his two monosyllabic neighbours and guffawed at the in-jokes about people and businesses in the neighbourhood. They applauded for the snowstorm, whooped as the two little girls in the cow costume were steered around stage and held their breath as a very frail man of eighty, playing the old Huron Indian, delivered the best laugh line of the night. They joined lustily in the carols at the end of the play and then trooped through the hall kitchen to demolish a dessert table set up by the churchwomen. We all had to agree it was a howling success.

Word travelled around the community next day, and by eight o'clock on the second night the parish hall was jammed. People stood in rows at the back, and children perched in the window wells, sat on their mothers' laps and crowded around the base of the stage on the floor. The actors were flushed with the success of their first comic hit, and it was all I could do to restrain them from rewriting the play with their ad libs.

In a time when most of our dealings with other people seem to be driven by impatience, I was reminded how rare it is for us to find something to work on together just for the fun of it. As I watched the faces in the audience on that last night of the play, it occurred to me that what we were doing was nothing new. This community still has a living memory of the days when it entertained itself just this way. The halls we use were all built with stages in them so that people could make their own fun after strawberry suppers, fowl suppers, agricultural meetings and church functions.

Since those two nights in mid-December, we have made fast friends of the people who participated in the play and often exchange little smiles with them about the moments we shared on stage. We remember the Angel of the Lord with wings, a halo and a bottle of beer sitting on the parish steps smoking a cigarette; how difficult it was to get the snowstorm crew stopped once they were wound up; and, at the climax of the play, when the hero and the cow hunkered down together in the snowstorm for the night, an indignant little voice from the back of the cow costume protested loudly, "You're sitting on me!"

And the best moment of all, when we flung open the doors of the overheated hall and realized that the snow had begun to fall in big, fat flakes. A lady turned to my wife with a wonderful smile and said, "It really is Christmas now!"

Home Remedies

I have been felled by a flu bug. I am now in bed surrounded by magazines and boxes of tissues, reflecting on the various strategies for disease management that prevail in this house and elsewhere on the concession roads. This particular bug has also toppled my own "apple a day" theory of disease prevention, which I resurrected from antiquity last spring and applied to myself. It worked for eight months, which is a reasonable stretch to go without a cold but not long enough to found a health cult and start a mail order business.

Fifty years ago a lot of the people who lived in the country thought you exposed yourself to the greatest risk of disease when you took a bath. Baths were "weakening," and most of the old farmers climbed into thermal underwear at Thanksgiving and shed it sometime after the Victoria Day weekend. Today the grandchildren of that superstitious but self-sufficient generation feel that you're most at risk of catching a cold on a flight back to Canada after snorkelling in Aruba.

There are, however, still pockets of the old thinking. In my wife's family the medicine shelf is not clearly divided between treatments for man and beast. Rawleigh's Ointment and Dr. Thomas' Eclectric Oil stand side by side with Bag Balm, horse liniment and pinkeye spray. The patents on some of these bottles go back to the 1840s, and there are cures here for everything from stubborn cases of staggers and the mange to more pernicious afflictions like tuberculosis, heart failure and blindness. No such claims are made on the container, of course, for this is now illegal. The claims are all made by the patients. But if I express any skepticism about these cures, there are knowing looks and patronizing nods around the table as if to say, "all book learning and no common sense."

When I fell and broke my heel last year, several young people in the neighbourhood dropped by with a variety of unguents and potions to apply and ingest. There was comfrey and boneset to promote the knitting of the bone, glucosamine and shark cartilage to promote the growth of new soft tissue. My cousin, a medical doctor who specializes in holistic medicine, raised his eyebrows when I mentioned shark cartilage. "It can lead to a rapid shrinking of the wallet," he warned and suggested I could get the same results by eating gelatine while looking at shark photographs.

Then someone sent me a bottle of earthworm powder. My cousin finally lost his patience. "How long do you suppose it would be before the College of Physicians and Surgeons came tapping on my door if I started prescribing infusions of earthworm powder for broken heels?"

I finally opted for a Scottish remedy that was developed shortly after the Battle of Culloden and has been used successfully in the treatment of smashed heels ever since. It was called a subtalar fusion, and I had it performed under general anaesthetic at St. Michael's Hospital last fall by a surgeon. Call me old-fashioned if you like, but the treatment was successful and now I'm walking again just fine.

In the court of Peter the Great, the Russian czar, no one dared complain of a toothache within earshot of the emperor, because he had a fascination with the science of dentistry and would drop everything to operate on you. I share the same caution around any of the women in my wife's family, including my own daughter.

If you sniffle in their company and fall into their clutches, they slap and pummel and rub you down vigorously with Rawleigh's,

Vick's and Dr. Thomas'. Then they infuse you with a mixture of eucalyptus/menthol/camphor inhalant under a hot wet towel, and finally they drench you with an iron tonic and fish paralyzer in a fine sherry base and put you to bed wrapped in hot flannel. After a treatment like this you feel and smell like you've just been rustproofed.

I lie here playing soldiers with the blankets, imagining the microbes fleeing my body like Highlanders escaping the musket fire of the British. I think I must be getting better.

The Visiting Season

For three months of every year Nottawasaga Township is like the south of France. A breeze off the lake freshens the air and sheep frolic in green pastures. During the rest of the year, though, it's like Nottawasaga Township. Struggling through seven months of the Great Canadian Dark in this part of the country requires more than a good recipe for bean soup and a couple of hotel weekends in the city. And for a family of six operating on a writer's income computed in declining Canadian dollars, the idea of a white sand beach in April must remain pretty much a pipe dream.

I admire those people who can lose themselves in winter sports, but after ten winters out here on the farm I have found that the key to mental health in heavy frost and low light is to maintain a sense of purpose and make regular efforts to seek out human community. Of course, this is not a novel idea. Social life in the countryside was originally organized around exactly this theme. Winter was the traditional visiting time, when roads were snow-packed and easier to travel and the work around the farm was lighter. Today the old farm population has all but disappeared, but many of the organizations it left behind still survive.

We tend to lean on two of the oldest institutions for relief: the Duntroon Anglican Church and the Collingwood Fair Board. We have also invented a new one: the Dallas Sideroad Literary Society. Membership in these three groups guarantees that you are never more than forty-eight hours away from a potluck supper. Together they serve as the emotional equivalent of a eucalyptus steam bath.

Last year the church held several suppers, a theatre excursion and a dozen planning sessions for the renovation of a schoolhouse for our new couples club and Sunday school. Right now we're up at the hall with crowbars and paintbrushes doing the work and planning a big fundraising dinner themed around the last dinner on the *Titanic*.

The fair board meets relentlessly all winter in regular monthly sessions, as an executive, in committees and work parties, most often with food, even if it's only a box of donuts and a coffee perk. The fall fair is still six months off, but we exhaust ourselves in debate, decision making and storytelling far into the night.

The literary society has no membership dues, no agenda and no constitution. Club meetings occur spontaneously, by invitation only, and are held around a large antique billiard table. There is only one rule and it is a firm one: any member who brings a book to the meeting will have his cue privileges retired.

In these months of low cumulus and long icicles, a lot of good work is being done across the higher latitudes of this country by citizens with a strong instinct for public service and their own diversion. There is one community I know of, about an hour southwest of us, that holds at least one dance in aid of fire victims every year. Last winter it came time for the dance, but there had been no fires so people went out and burned down a small shed to give the evening official standing. I know a small group of manic farmers in the Rockwood area who take a pause from playing elaborate practical jokes on one another to hold a March Blahs dance for the community. Hundreds turn out to see them tell awful jokes in a joke booth, sing songs and put on macabre displays of line dancing. The place is always packed and proceeds go to local charities. In a few weeks the sound of rushing water in the ditches will signal the end of the visiting season. We will stumble outside, blinking like groundhogs in the bright sunshine, grateful to these groups for our mental health and ready to face a growing season full of promise.

Name Dropping

There was a scene in *The Culpepper Cattle Co.*, a 1970s western, in which the grizzled cowboy rides toward the saloon at a dead gallop, skids to a halt in a cloud of dust and steps smoothly off the horse right onto the boardwalk. A little kid watches him from the saloon doors and asks, "What's your horse's name, mister?" Without breaking stride the cowboy replies, "You don't put a name on something you might have to eat, son."

As I remember, that cowboy didn't live on a small farm with four young kids, as I do. You can't follow rules like that in the spring of the year when the sheep are lambing and the cows are calving and the children are hanging over the stable door watching the earth bring forth its increase.

Up till recently the older kids relied on Walt Disney videos for inspiration, and the barn has been populated by personalities like Jasmine, Ariel, Linsey-Woolsey, Dopey and Sneezy. But now they've begun reaching further afield into pop culture, and we have Kramer the Rooster, Leonardo di Capon and, briefly last summer, Bouchard and Parizeau, the freezer pigs.

I used to name the horned milking goats after famous suffragettes like Mrs. Pankhurst, Mrs. Stanton and Mrs. Anthony. They were the opinion leaders of the barnyard, knocking unconscious any other animal that crossed them in debate or at the feed trough. I thought they made excellent role models for my daughters, but Madeline, who is now nine, has rechristened them the Spice Goats: Lily Spice, Sassy Spice, Leona Spice, Jumpy Spice and Old Spice. This is fine with me. A goat by any other name would smell as sweet. Besides, Goat Power is something everybody can identify with around here, especially Bingo, the billy goat who has several large bumps on his head to show for his failure to grasp key concepts about The Movement.

Last fall our next-door neighbour Susy, who just started teaching high school, brought me three baby chicks her class hatched as a science project. I was the logical place to get rid of them, because I keep forty hens in a henhouse out in the orchard. When the chicks arrived, I was a little busy so I just put them in a cardboard box on my desk and turned the lamp over them for heat. There they stayed for about a month, until the ladies who come to clean the house every week (Flora, Fauna and Merriwether) commented that my office smelled like a chicken coop. We moved the chicks to the feed room of the henhouse and put them under a proper brooder.

The chicks grew up and feathered out over the next six months, turning into giant tan-coloured birds who tower over the little factory-order brown and white hens I get from the Stayner Feed Service every spring. Even so, the older hens attacked the lumbering giants each time I tried to introduce them to the flock. They continue to be restricted to separate quarters in the feed room. It soon became apparent that there were two roosters and one hen, and one of the roosters began attacking the kids when they went in to collect the eggs. So we sent him down to my mother-in-law, who had been looking for a rooster to help keep her henhouse running smoothly.

The other two have turned into a rather charming couple, and the children have named them Sophie and Kramer. The hen is large, bosomy and very calm. She follows me about, stepping carefully and clucking softly. Whenever you stoop down to pat her she hunches her shoulders as though a grand piano is about to fall on her. But then she settles quietly and lets you stroke her feathers. The rooster is a very showy weathervane-type barnyard rooster with a bright red comb, multicoloured hackles and a magnificent tail that reminds me of the wake of a water skier. He has a permanently startled look, as though he just remembered some parcels he left on the subway, and he leaps about a foot off the ground whenever you come around a corner unexpectedly. In the morning when the feed room door is opened, he does one of the great stage entrances of all time, rushing out into the light and stopping suddenly as though he has incredible news to tell.

I suppose it is a risk to give name and character to a potential Sunday dinner entrée, but by the time I get tired of Kramer, he'll be too old to eat.

Pig Tales

One of the luxuries of running a hobby farm is the ability to experiment with a new idea without putting the whole enterprise at risk and courting financial disaster.

Two years ago I read about a farmer in Kentucky named Joel Salatin, who stumbled onto a neat way to fatten cattle and pigs in the same space and turn out compost at the same time. The man observed that animals graze in a specific order—cattle after sheep, pigs after cattle, chickens after all three—and he decided to put their natural tendencies to work. He fattened a few steers in the barnyard through the winter and sprinkled a bag of whole barley into the manure pack every week. When the cattle went out in the spring, he put a dozen pigs into the same space and watched them root through the manure pack looking for fermented grain. By the time the hogs were fat he had a ton of lovely black compost that was perfect for his market garden.

This all struck me as a brilliant idea, so I spread whole grain over the manure pack in my loafing shed under the Duchess and Rosie and went to my neighbour, Archie Currie, to ask him if he would sell me a couple of weaner pigs.

Archie frowned and shook his head. "I don't like to do that, as a rule," he said. I presumed he was reluctant to part with six-week-old pigs because there isn't much profit for him at that size and he preferred to raise them up to two hundred pounds to make a decent return.

"No, that's not the reason," said Archie. "Every time I sell a man weaner pigs, his wife gets pregnant."

I laughed and told him there really wasn't anything to worry about on that account. So, Archie hauled two forty-pound pigs out of the pen and put them in the box on the back of my old Ford truck, and I took them home to conduct this great experiment in symbiotic livestock management and compost production.

It worked like a charm. The pigs settled in quickly and by the end of the week they were enthusiastically snooting up the manure pack and romping around the barnyard like good, happy pigs. Within a month I was carting wheelbarrows of compost to the garden and watching super corn plants shoot up into the sky. The pigs escaped from the barnyard several times, usually because I had forgotten to fasten the gate, but they travelled only a few yards before they lay down and fell asleep, once on the cool concrete of the barn floor, another time under the henhouse. I finally let them out into the pasture with the cows, and there they stayed until the fall, munching on grounder apples, rooting up the topsoil and trotting cheerfully up to the barn whenever I came with their morning ration of pellets.

I had to resort to base treachery to get them off to market. During the last week in September I began putting their breakfast in the same crate I had used to bring them over from Archie's. On the first day of October I banged the door shut on them, hoisted the crate onto the Ford with a chain and front-end loader and drove them over to Hoffman's, in Stayner.

It was lonely in the barnyard with the pigs gone. I remembered the same feeling years ago as a child at my mother's farm when the pigs went out in the fall and the frost lay heavy on the empty troughs and feeders in the yard. But this time it was different. As the nights grew colder, the Duchess and Rosie came back up to the barnyard with their calves, and I could see that we had found a natural cycle that would repeat again and again. Moments like these come as close to perfection as any that can be found in a place as chaotic as a farm. In this little circle there is economy, not much work, bacon, beef and compost. There seems to be something in it for everybody, even the pigs, if I may presume to speak for them. They enjoy a lifestyle that is not available to the average bacon hog these days, and they have only one bad day.

I reflected on the success of the venture to my wife as we leaned on the barnyard gate and watched the cows munch on a large round bale. She agreed but said she doubted that Archie would sell us more weaner pigs next year.

"Why is that?" I asked.

"I'm pregnant," she said.

The Old Farm Truck

H ere at the farm we don't need a truck that will go anywhere every day. We just need something that can make it to the dump and back without attracting the attention of the transport officials.

I drive a 1983 Ford F-150 that was retired from the Hamilton Construction fleet nine years ago after clicking over the two-hundred-thousand-kilometre mark. I paid twelve hundred dollars for it, put new tires, shocks, a muffler and wipers on it, fixed the brakes, gave it a tune-up and painted it bright red. My brother-in-law, the cash crop farmer who was driving a twenty-five-thousand-dollar black diesel pickup at the time, studied the finished result and shook his head. "You sure do like old stuff," was all he would say. After it was repaired and licensed and ready for the road, I didn't bother with collision insurance, believing, as Hughie the farmer next door does, that "you shouldn't drive anything you can't afford to walk away from."

I like the clean, square lines of this truck, a style that was long ago discarded in favour of the current urban cowboy look. She has the three-hundred-cubic-inch straight-six engine, which Ford used with little or no change for more than thirty years, and a number of endearing traits. For the first few months every spring you have to pop the hood, remove the air filter and squirt gas in the carburetor to get her to fire up, but by the time the hot weather comes she starts on her own with just a couple of dozen pumps of the accelerator pedal. There's a leak on the top of the windshield on the passenger side, but this is not a problem because I seldom drive in the rain and few people care to be seen riding with me. The signal from CBC fades in and out on the old radio, depending on which side of the Duntroon hill we are on. I open the tailgate with an old lawnmower blade, and the ignition has been turned so many times that it no longer needs the key, which is very handy when the neighbours need the loan of a truck. (Last month, after driving without a key for six years, I found myself stranded at a local gas station when the old Ford made a sudden decision to beef up security, much like the RCMP at Sussex Drive.)

Over the last nine years I've loaded her to impossible heights with hay and straw in the back field, moved furniture for friends, hauled loads of wood down the steep back roads of the Niagara Escarpment from the Grey Forest, cedar rails from all points of the compass and, of course, uncounted loads to the township dump. I've brought animals and equipment home from auctions, trundled unfortunate sheep and pigs to the slaughterhouse, delivered loads of straw and manure to friends and taken kids for evening joyrides through the fields. To minimize salt damage I try not to drive her in the winter, but at rest she still gives service as an extra workbench and cutting surface while parked beside the barn workshop. And her gunwales are the perfect height for supporting the elbows of neighbours and friends while we sort out difficult political matters and tell stories.

I broke my foot a couple of years ago and didn't drive the old truck for a long time. When I finally took her out last spring, she was looking very tired. The brakes were grinding and she sagged on one corner with a broken coil spring. I reluctantly decided that her days were done and drove her over to the wrecker, who just shrugged and offered me twenty-five dollars for her. I stood there for a few minutes, thinking, while he dealt with another customer and traffic whizzed by on the highway. Then, driven by one of those strange impulses that strike me about every forty-eight hours around here, I climbed back in the truck and drove home to the farm.

Since then I have replaced the brakes, coil spring, tie-rod ends, radiator and most of the hoses. My neighbourhood welder has patched the holes over the wheel wells with replacement panels and covered them in black paint. I even replaced the main seal to stop a hemorrhage of oil.

"Folly," says my brother-in-law from the window of his new silver forty-thousand-dollar pickup and shakes his head, but I am too far gone to listen to good advice. A two-tone truck with welded replacement panels is a magnet for the highway patrol, so I am sending her over to Hutchison Light Truck next week for new front fenders and a professional paint job. Red, of course, with maybe a silver racing stripe down the side. Then we'll replace the door seals and perhaps find a radio that will draw in at least the Collingwood station.

My brother-in-law is right. I like old stuff . . . and I love this truck.

School's Out

There is no joy on the concession road this morning. We woke to news that our county school board has announced a list of schools slated for closure, including our public school in the little village of Duntroon up the hill. The children are all to be put on buses and sent down the road to the new public school in Nottawa, on the outskirts of Collingwood.

The news doesn't come as a shock, really, although it has put a damper on our rehearsals for the Christmas play at the church. You see, board officials have been telling us for several years that the school is an inefficient size, the septic system is at capacity, the "economies of scale" aren't working for us and we are "high cost." They point to a set of drawings for the ideal school that have apparently been etched into the pink granite walls of the new fifteen-million-dollar County Education Centre, forty miles away in Barrie, and say that to be efficient today we really should be serving four hundred children, not a hundred and sixty.

The officials agree that there is actually nothing wrong with the building. It is structurally sound, clean, quiet and fun to work in for the teachers and students. In fact, just a year ago, in a most peculiar burst of interest, the board descended on the school and spent a hundred thousand dollars to install a new air-conditioning system. We were a little surprised by this because it seemed like a lot of money to spend on a building you're going to abandon. And besides, Duntroon is a breezy location on the Niagara Escarpment and the air quality is actually pretty good. The thermostats are now controlled from Barrie, and sometimes they get a warm front over there while it's still blowing cold off the lake up here, and the kids have to put on their coats while someone makes a long-distance call to Barrie. So we're pretty philosophical about the board's idea of efficiency.

The septic tank works fine too, unless you're a school board building superintendent working from nitrate-loading tables written in 1974 by a grizzled old sewage plant engineer from the Water Resources Commission. That old engineer, if he's still alive, would be flattered to know that someone somewhere was still using that table today, although I think he'd be upset to know it was being used to kick kids out of a rural village and bus them down the road into town. He would probably point at the herd of cattle in the pasture across the road and observe that ten of those cows dump more nitrate on the field in an afternoon than a hundred and sixty kids put in the septic tank on Friday Pizza Day, and no one would consider busing those cows into town. I mean, that wouldn't make sense, even to a school board.

No, the real problem is that we're not big enough and therefore we cannot be allowed to continue to operate. Yes, it will be expensive to move us and no, there is presently no room at the new school in town, but they're telling us that they'll put portables on the site and then we can start talking about spending a million dollars or so to put an addition on the new school. As I say, it always takes us a little longer than the experts to discover where the savings will be found in all of this.

Ironically enough, I'm sitting on the veranda of the old red schoolhouse across the road from Duntroon Public School, putting the last touches on the Christmas play. The old school was built in 1879, replacing a log schoolhouse from the 1830s that stood around the corner, the first school built west of the Nottawasaga River. The red school was closed in the 1960s when the provincial government shut down all the local school boards and moved to the county system. It served as a township municipal office for thirty years until yet another restructuring shut the municipal office down too.

Sitting here I reflect on the links the school has forged with the community around it: with the daycare centre next door, with the community hall and the baseball diamond up the street, with Jack Swalm's Basement Pioneer Museum of Duntroon and, in complex and mysterious ways, with almost every one of the small businesses and forty-odd houses that cluster around these corners.

I begin to understand that the policy that does away with yet another generation of rural schools could only be written under fluorescent lights in a place far away by people who have no idea what holds a rural community together, by people whose way of listening to you has become their way of ignoring you.

And I decide that it's a shame our energies can't be harnessed to a more useful purpose, like improving the place where we live.

No Cows for Alarm

I 've never been that fond of beef cattle. They're big, clumsy animals with small brains, large appetites and absolutely zero interest in personal hygiene. Most cows are guided by three rules in life: if it moves, run away from it; if it doesn't move, knock it over; and if you can't knock it over, poop on it. It never occurred to me to keep any here on the farm.

I always preferred dairy cows. We had a few Jerseys when I was a kid, the gentle, tan-coloured cows that give milk so rich you can feel your arteries hardening as you drink it. They're smaller and finer boned and much calmer than beef cattle, although dairy cows are also capable of property damage in close quarters. I used to bring them up from the bottom pasture in the quiet of the evening, following their swaying backsides along the sand track in my bare feet, smelling that fermented grass–milk smell of them mixed with the cool tang of the cedars that lined the rail fences.

There were some struggles getting them to be led by a halter, and the odd leg rope was needed when breaking in a new recruit to hand-milking, but generally they submitted to our demands patiently. And they could be tricked more often than a Canadian voter. In the heat of the summer, when the flies were bad, a cow's eye might start to water and half-close, so you bought an aerosol can of pinkeye spray from the Co-op and went out into the field, sat down in the grass and waited. Eventually, the cow would come over to visit and see if something needed to be knocked over or pooped on. You showed the spray can to her, she tilted her head and looked with great interest right down the barrel and you pulled the trigger. You only got one chance, but if you missed or had to do the other eye, she would forget about it by next day and you could spring the trap on her all over again.

Some of the sweetest memories of my childhood are from those summers at the farm, running through the house-high hay and napping in the heat of the afternoon under a shade tree with a flabby old moo as a pillow. So when we moved back to the farm, I decided to re-create the magic for my own children and tracked down the last descendant of my mother's old herd, an eleven-year-old hornless beast named Roxy, who gave bathtubs of that rich milk of my youth.

Unfortunately the children didn't take to Roxy milk. They'd all been raised on goat's milk and found the Jersey milk much too rich, even when it was separated. I milked Roxy for a year, sharing the milk with the dogs and the cats and the chickens until we were all popping Rolaids tablets before bedtime. Roxy eventually went dry, raised one more calf and then expired, bringing my dairy experiment to a close.

The same year Old George, a colourful local cattle baron, drove up to my gate the week before Christmas and unloaded a little Belted Galloway heifer that looked like an Oreo cookie with four feet. The Galloway is a marginal breed, smaller than the present fashion in beef and always sniffed at and discounted heavily at the stockyards, but it is an easy keeper and generally docile. George said he wanted me to be the spokesman for the Nottawasaga Township Galloway Association, an organization whose membership would double if I would agree to join.

"You can't just give her to me," I protested.

"Of course I can," George boomed. "It's Christmas!"

And so we are beef farmers, although nothing has as yet made its way to the freezer. There are four out there now: Duchess, Jasmine, Miss Moo and Anastasia. I named the last one myself in the forlorn hope she might go to the "House of Special Purpose," but George and my wife object to sending a good cow out for meat. They're all as tame as spaniels and come romping across the field whenever I show my face on the veranda and call, "Co-Boss!"

My two-year-old daughter and four-year-old son spent much of last fall sitting under an apple tree, poking apples through the rail fence into the waiting maws of the mother cows, watching their long sandpaper tongues wind around the fruit and listening for the deep, satisfying crunch as it found its way back to the molars. By the enchanted look on the kids' faces I assume that they too are warming to the idea of beef farming.

The Bun Burn in the Bush

At this time of the year I am always startled and amazed to hear families tell me about travel plans they have made to Caribbean beaches and ski villas in Quebec. I leaf through the same brochures hopefully each year, but the idea of leaving the pipes in the barn to the care of a volunteer in winter defeats me every time. Even if we had the seven thousand dollars, and even if we could put everybody, including the goose, on a self-feeder, there is no place in the vacation world where they actually want to deal with a family of four kids.

My wife and I have learned that to stay sane in the country in the cruellest months of late winter you need the leadership skills of a Shackleton or a Franklin. And we rely heavily on traditions like the annual Bun Burn in the Bush.

Our first Bun Burn happened almost by accident, about seven years ago. One morning in foul weather during the March Break down at my wife's family farm, in the windy hills of Mulmur Township, we were sitting around the house trying to watch a movie in an overheated living room. The children and their cousins, however, were trying out for the national bed-jumping Olympic team, and we had to push the pause button several times to treat lacerations. The noise was incredible. We were dangerously close to a case of the "shack nasties," a condition that strikes many rural homes across the country about this time of the year.

Out of the blue my brother-in-law, Kerry, said, "Why don't we take the kids for a walk down to the river?"

I blinked and looked out the window doubtfully. The police had closed the highways because of high winds and freezing rain. The little lane down the hill through the pasture to the river was clogged with huge soggy snowdrifts. Broken ice branches dropped from the trees and clattered on the ground outside. It's hard enough to make the kids stay out for ten minutes on days like this, but before I could speak up my wife said, "That's a great idea. We could make it a picnic."

This suggestion had an electric effect on the company. The children dove for their coats and boots, and Kerry went out to the drive shed to fire up his little antique bulldozer. He hooked on an old manure spreader he uses for hauling wood and threw a roll of carpet and some straw bales in it for the kids to sit on. We bundled the kids up in their snowsuits and stuffed them into the spreader along with a hamper full of hot dogs and pop. Then, with ice already forming on my glasses, we set off down the unopened road allowance that leads to the Boyne River.

The wind screamed around us as we made the heart-stopping descent, the bulldozer sliding sideways on icy patches, making the spreader bounce off fence posts and producing shrieks of excitement from the children. This was early in the marriage, before I had become accustomed to the casual confidence with which my in-laws move machinery up and down these hills.

On the flats below, the wind dropped abruptly as we entered the cedar bush. We churned through the rotten snow to a clearing on the riverbank, and the bulldozer sputtered to a halt. For a brief moment everything was still. I could see the treetops swaying quietly above us, but here on the ground the air was still and quite pleasant. The children watched for a moment in silence as large snowflakes floated down to the water and disappeared.

Then they exploded out of the spreader, and the festivities began. We rolled out the carpet on the riverbank for the babies to crawl around on. The older cousins and aunts went off to look for fish along the river. The husbands started a bonfire, carved marshmallow sticks and prepared the lunch. Before long we were all comfortably lolling about on the carpet munching charred hot dogs, peeling fried marshmallows off the babies' snowsuits and telling stories of our youth. We stayed down there all afternoon, and when we got finally got back the children watched a movie and fell asleep.

The Bun Burn is now in its eighth year and has become a by-invitation-only event.

Making Time Fly

I have been down on my hands and knees digging in the garden for much of the day, far too early for this part of the country, but the breeze is gentle and from the south, the Baltimore orioles have returned to the old pear tree and the sun is coaxing the last of the frost out of the clods I turned up with the plow last fall. It's the sort of day a disciplined writer is supposed to ignore, but I rose above my work ethic and opted for a day of puttering.

Carl Jung told us that if we want to know what we should be doing with our lives, we should look back to our childhood and try to remember what it was we did that made time fly. I remember a sandbank beside the farm lane where I played for years, marking out farms, villages and roads and populating them with plastic animals and figures. My Wingfield Farm stage plays about Persephone Township came out of the same mental sandbox, and the work I have done on them has given me as much satisfaction as any of the earlier occupations I forced on myself as an economics student, journalist, speechwriter and public relations officer.

The other thing that makes time fly for me is puttering. My wife understands that from time to time I will feel the need to drag some ancient piece of machinery out of the fencerow and tear it apart in an attempt to make it work again. Last summer, I tripped over a coulter that fell off the Massey trip plow five years ago when I was preparing the field for a crop of grain. The plow was given to me as a wedding present by an old friend, now deceased, and the work I did knocking the sand out of the coulter, greasing and making it spin again, and restoring it to its place on the plow gave me as much satisfaction as anything I might have achieved on paper in the same time. Puttering reassures me about many things: that the past is not entirely lost, that there are still some mechanical processes that can be understood and that I don't have to shop for entertainment.

In my wife's family the women all have a remarkable tolerance for a man's need to putter, which offers one explanation for the success of their marriages going back several generations. There was a grandfather who might have become a failed and bitter farmer if he had not been allowed to turn his love of firearms and gun repair into a lifelong hobby and craft, which evolved into the Creemore Gun Club. He put up a shooting range on a corner of the farm and, over the course of thirty years, built a huge and devoted circle of friends and admirers who still cannot speak of him without a tremor in their voice and misty eyes.

Today if a man in that family is replacing a broken key on an accordion, or stitching new glass eyes onto a moosehead he picked up at a yard sale, or out in the shop tearing down a lawn-mower engine to power a turnip shredder even though he stopped growing turnips in 1968, his wife will explain with a shrug and a quiet smile that he is "busy" and make up a plate of food for him. These are moments I find quite moving, rooted as they are in toler-ance, affection and a deep understanding of a man's need to seek the dream state that can be found only at a workbench in a cloud of WD-40 fumes.

I used to achieve similar moments out on the Pretty River with a fly rod and a lunch pail full of ham sandwiches and Newcastle Browns, but now, with four children and five dogs who all love the water and the riverbank jammed with a new generation of sport fishermen kitted out from L.L. Bean catalogues, I have given it up.

This afternoon my trowel struck hard on a large iron object. It turned out to be the head off a First World War trenching spade, probably left here by one of the Currie family who gardened in this spot back in the 1960s. An overnight in the Varsol bath, a good scrub and a coat of black Tremclad paint will make it as good as new. I'm sure there's a spade handle around here somewhere . . .

Country Etiquette

I t must be daunting for a city person of average goodwill to land in a place like Nottawasaga Township and try to make sense of the language, the rituals and the taboos of rural life. As a transplant myself, I think I am qualified to act as a guide to the newly arrived, offering useful tips on country etiquette and pointing out the holes and hazards.

The first rule, of course, is to be careful what you say about people, because they're all related. After that, it's mostly a question of language.

In the country a lunch is the meal they serve at a funeral or at midnight after a dance or a good visit. The meal in the middle of the day is called dinner and the evening meal is called supper. If you cross the threshold at either of these times, you're automatically invited to sit down with the family. If you feel the urge to reciprocate, this is good, but forget the city custom of inviting people over for drinks before supper and then throwing them out with nothing to eat. This is more than puzzling to a country person. It conflicts sharply with his views about hospitality (and her views about temperance too).

Some farmers I know prefer not to be telephoned during the noon hour. They like to sit down over their lunch (dinner) without interruption, especially during busy times like the seeding and harvest. If you want to talk to them, it's better just to drive over and drop in, whatever the time of day or year. Then they'll lean on the box of the pickup and talk to you all afternoon.

It's fine to talk crops and the weather, but be careful not to say anything about a farmer's crop that might be taken as criticism. A careless remark about weeds will hang in the air for years to come. On the other hand don't enthuse about a crop that is still in the ground, because this might bring bad luck. The countryside is still an Evil Eye culture, always looking over its shoulder at vengeful gods. Obviously this leaves a very narrow window of opportunity for small talk about crops, which is why the farmers themselves talk to one another in such mind-numbing technical detail about corn heat units and herbicide rates, or leave the subject altogether and move on to the weather.

A lot has been written about the rural wave. The Japanese tea ceremony is an uncomplicated affair compared with this business of knowing when to wave, how often in the same day, whether to engage the arm at the shoulder, elbow or wrist, or when a simple straightening of one index finger on the steering wheel will do. Certain situations require more than a wave, such as a roadside breakdown attended by three or more persons all known to the driver or an escaped cow being chased by three children and a pregnant woman.

When city people arrive the first thing they do is slap up a lot of No Trespassing signs around the property. All these signs ever do is persuade your neighbours that you are standoffish. Trespassers and messy picnickers can be controlled with a sign that says "Beware of Snakes." But in time you will learn, as I have, that a figure walking across your field is more of a reason to put the kettle on than to call the police.

The country was made for visits. Rail fences and pickup truck boxes are designed at just the right height so you can put your elbows over them, lean and yarn with a neighbour for an hour or so. Mailboxes draw people to a fixed point at roughly the same time every day. Shady verandas beckon you to an empty chair in the heat of the afternoon. The diner in the village is the sort of restaurant where you don't look for a table, you just find a chair.

None of this is coincidence. The old rural community was built on an elaborate system of shared work and play that revolved around a seasonal timetable and was knit together by visits and stories. Evidence of that old code still appears in the speech and manners of the residents in the same way old barn foundations and stone fences poke through the landscape. And the great irony is that, as society restructures around home-based occupations and more and more people return to the sideroads to rebuild on the old foundations, they find themselves rediscovering the ancient art of neighbouring.

A Norman Rockwell Christmas

L ast year I read about a new place to take the family for a U-pick Christmas tree, so I raised the idea at the supper table one night.

"What's the matter with the place we always go?" asked my wife.

"Nothing at all," I said. "It's just that the new place is closer, they have the sleigh ride, the cider and the bonfire. Why drive twenty miles when we have the same thing next door?"

"Do they have spruce?" asked my eleven-year-old daughter, Madeline. Spruce is very important to the women in my family. They would no more put a Scotch pine in the living room than they would serve instant mashed potatoes for Christmas dinner.

"It says here they have all varieties," I said.

"We should try it," announced Hart, who is nine, and an explorer like myself. Matthew, who is five, seconded the motion. Hannah, who is two, banged her spoon on the high chair and shouted, "Punkin!"

On Sunday morning after church we set off in the van along the muddy concession road to a sign at the top of the hill announcing "Xmas Tree U-pick" and turned down a bumpy lane into a parking lot in front of a barn. There were a few trees in piles, but, ominously, none of them were spruce.

A woman in a Santa hat appeared and assured us they had spruce at the back of the farm. Twenty minutes later the horses appeared, we all got comfortable on the straw bales and lurched off, the boys singing "Jingle Bells" at the top of their lungs and the baby laughing all the way. The sun peeked through damp clouds and a gentle wind rustled the dead thistles beside the lane.

When we got to the main tree lot, the owner told us we'd find a row of spruce along the line fence up the hill. "Follow the row north to the maple bush and you'll find more of them." We walked up the hill to the line fence and found a row of spruce about three feet high. Heath and Madeline looked at me.

"This is supposed to be a Christmas tree?" they asked, in unison. We followed the row to the maple bush and turned west. The trees started to get bigger and our hopes rose. Then they got smaller again. I paused for a moment beside a four-footer, but Heath said, "Don't even think about it." We were now deep into the second farm, my shoulders were getting tired from carrying Hannah and I was starting to wheeze. The row turned abruptly south, a long row of knee-high spruces as far as the eye could see. We trudged on. At the crest of a hill, the row petered out and stopped altogether. At the very end stood a lone spruce, a bit lop-sided and somewhat drought stricken but noticeably higher than anything we had seen so far. We stood there panting and considered that tree for a long moment. I chose my words carefully.

"We're now a half-hour walk from the horses. The horses are a half-hour from the car and the car is twenty-five miles from the other tree place. Do you think we can live with this tree?"

"It looks okay to me, Dad," said Hart cheerfully. Matthew agreed.

"It's awful," said Maddie flatly.

"Spoose!" said Hannah.

"Cut it," said Heath evenly.

Down came the tree. Hart and I each grabbed a lower branch and struck off through the brush in the general direction of home. Behind us the air turned blue as Maddie found thirty different adjectives for the tree.

Back at the farm we sprayed the tree with the hose to make it green again. Bolted into a tree stand it looked much more respectable and considerably taller. An hour later, with forty pounds of electric lights, tinsel and ornaments, it looked pretty much like any tree we'd ever had. That night we sat in the glow of the lights with Hannah nestled in between us.

"It's actually one of our nicest trees," my wife conceded.

"Crimmus!" said Hannah, happily.

I'll never take a risk like that again.

Hawk among the Chickens

I n the days when I worked for a large insurance company in
the city and rode the subway to work, my observations about
the outdoors were limited to whether or not I needed to wear a
coat. Today in the short walk from the house to the barn I absorb
enough information to carry the conversation over morning coffee.

I check the thermometer on the veranda, sniff the air and
glance over to Blue Mountain, which brings us all our weather. I
note automatically whether the wind is up or down, what direction
it's coming from and the height of the clouds. A deer strolls along
the fence line in the winter wheat. Pigs squeal in the barn across
the road as breakfast is served. A red-tailed hawk screams in the
distance, circling over the bush at the back of the farm.

Country people watch the natural world as closely as market
analysts track consumer spending and trade statistics. This is a
natural human response whenever large and potentially dangerous
forces range against us.

The information I take special note of today is that the hawk is
still here and my hens must remain inside. They've been confined
to barracks for three months now because of him. He made off
with four hens in September before I noticed that something was
amiss. Every couple of days I'd find a few loose feathers wafting

about in the orchard, and the count would be short another hen at bedtime. One afternoon I caught him red-handed, tearing apart a buff-coloured hen named Sophie that I had raised from a chick in a box on my desk. The hawk departed in haste, swooping under the apple trees to stay under the radar. Then he flew up to the top branch of a dead elm tree out in the sheep pasture where he waited for me to return to the house.

"Why don't you just shoot the bugger?" asked my wife.

I have never shot a hawk because they are such graceful, wild creatures, but this one had murdered an old pal, and Old Testament instincts surged through my veins. I buried Sophie and searched out the other hens, one by one, from their hiding places in the tall grass along the rail fence and returned them to the safety of the henhouse. In the reflective calm of the veranda swing chair, nursing a gin and tonic, I decided to keep the hens confined until the hawk flew south. The snow came and stayed and so did the hawk.

I called my good friend Dr. George Peck of Thornbury, who is a respected authority on the nesting birds of Ontario, and explained the situation. George said that this was unusual behaviour for the slow-moving red-tail.

"Are you sure it wasn't a goshawk?" he asked.

"No," I said. "We've got him on videotape."

George then informed me solemnly that red-tails don't fly south. That meant the problem wasn't going to fly away.

"What am I supposed to do?"

I already knew the answer. George is an ardent conservationist, a pacifist, and his advice is always of the uncompromising New Testament variety. Forgive the hawk and keep the hens in protective custody. In time he'll have to return to his regular diet of mice. But George surprised me.

"He shouldn't be doing that," he said. "Why don't you shoot the bugger?"

That left me alone with a moral dilemma, until Kenny Jardine came by with the mail.

"A hawk has been killing chickens all the way up the sideroad," he said. "There's a price on his head. People have been blasting at him for weeks."

"But hawks are a protected species," I protested.

"Yep, and chickens are pretty well protected too," said Kenny. "I give him another week, at the most."

I never saw the hawk again. The moral problem was taken out of my hands.

A Restoration Project

I have two tractors. One is a shiny green 1952 two-cylinder John Deere AR tractor that was lovingly restored by Bill Day of Creemore. Heath and I bought it with our wedding money in 1987. On my fortieth birthday she bought me another "Johnny Popper," a very shabby 1953 Model 40 that we found languishing on a dealer's lot in Elora, Ontario.

The AR is pretty but can't do anything but pull things. The 40 is much more versatile. It has a hydraulic loader on the front for lifting and scooping and a three-point hitch on the back for a lift plow, a snow blower or a wood splitter. It has performed light duties around the farm since 1991. Once a week during the winter it struggles from the main barn to the sheep barn with a round bale. Twice a year I use it to shovel out the stable and barnyard. The rest of the time it does odd jobs like grading the lane, dragging a dead tree or lifting a fence post out of the ground. In July both tractors come out to bring in the hay. On the weekend of the fair I drive the AR over to take part in the antique tractor show, but the 40 always stays home, like Cinderella, because it is so shabby.

I'm fond of them both, but they are not very reliable. They often sigh heavily and quit in the middle of a project, usually crossways in the middle of the sideroad or in front of the family car just before a piano lesson. When this happens you just have to sit down and isolate the problem (usually electrical) by process of elimination. I am fortunate to have married into a family that collects these machines like Blue Willow china, and its members are always happy to offer a telephone diagnosis for stubborn problems.

Over the last few years the 40 has been showing its age, growling in first gear because of a failed bearing and dripping oil from various points. The brakes are long gone, and my wife got a bad scare the day it popped out of gear while pulling a full manure spreader up a hill. I watched for eight heart-stopping seconds as she rolled back down the hill and crunched safely into a rail fence.

That was when I decided it was time for a "major mechanical." In September I drove it down to Lightheart Repairs, a little shop in the hills south of Stayner where the Lightheart brothers perform reconstructive surgery on the ancient treasures of the township. I call it the Combustion Club because whenever I drop in, at least ten vehicles are parked in the lane and a dozen or so visitors sit in a circle around the stove drinking Garnet's terrible coffee while they meditate over the correct firing order of a flathead six.

"A couple of months," they predicted, but these things develop a life of their own. On the operating table, Ralph and Garnet found a few other signs of pathology besides the faulty brakes and ancient transmission. They tightened the steering, repaired a slow leak in the gas tank, replaced seals, welded a leaky tire rim, put new leathers in the hydraulics, found a new grill and replaced the radiator core. By this time the 40 was in pieces all over the floor of the shop. Then we decided to paint it.

As Ralph says, "It's hard to know when to stop." He sent away for new gauges for the instrument panel and a complete decal package. He even built a new seat.

In a short but moving ceremony at the end of January the Lighthearts presented me with the key and a bill, which was quite reasonable considering the complexity of the task. Cinderella arrived home in triumph on Bob Ransier's trailer and took her rightful place beside the AR, a thing of beauty now and much improved utility.

This year, they go to the fair together.

You Don't Say

M y adopted home as a child was a hundred-acre farm on the Seventh Concession of a hilly township in central Ontario. Scots and Irish farmers originally settled the land, and some of their descendants still spoke a few words of Gaelic as late as the 1960s. Their speech was peppered with odd phrases and pronunciations that made them endlessly fascinating to a nine-year-old from North Toronto.

I was often asked to help "redd up the dishes" or fetch a shovel that was leaning up "firninst the fence." A thin cow was "gant" and a day with no wind was "cam." The barnyard was full of exotic creatures like "springers" (year-old heifers), "wethers" (castrated rams) and "yo-lambs" (young females). Animals, the weather and the natural world provided an inexhaustible source of colourful metaphor. An old horse that wouldn't trot was "slow as a day's rain" and a cow that kicked was in need of "a hardwood shampoo." At the end of a visit your host might offer to "see you past the gander" and caution you to "keep her between the fences" on the way home.

If you looked glum, someone might say you were in "a bit of a moult" but console you with the prediction that you would more than likely "get your feathers back" before long.

Every statement of fact was punctuated with the phrase "so it is" or "so you are" as if a snort of contradiction was on its way from the listener.

They all had a maddening reluctance to offer a straight yes or no to a direct question. "Mebbe" met all situations and conferred a much smaller liability on the speaker. My mother's explanation for this was that the Gaelic language of their ancestors had no single word for yes or no. Whether this was true or not, the words had long since fallen into disuse in my township.

The men swore in complete sentences and could use the pluperfect subjunctive with great facility if a wrench slipped and tore the skin off a knuckle. Inanimate objects were invested with vivid personalities and assumed to be hatching some sinister plot that would delay, inconvenience or cause personal injury, as in the following exchange between a pail of nails perched on a wiggly sawhorse and the farmer:

Pail of nails: Crash!

Farmer: Well then go ahead and fall down you miserable, two-toned, pie-eyed son of a *#$%!

If an operation did go according to plan, like the successful loading of a mad cattlebeast, it was said to be as "fine as frog's fur." If it failed because the little guy with the glasses couldn't hang onto the gate and the animal disappeared over the horizon in a cloud of dust, they would shake their heads and laugh that having me help was "like having two good men not show up."

The fences were flimsy, the machinery was ancient, many of the men drank heavily and the rest were alcoholics. It was certainly no paradise, and many people found that a wintry sense of humour helped to soften life's blows.

In a drought, conditions might become so desperate that "a grasshopper couldn't get across that field without a canteen." The resulting crop might be so poor that the grasshoppers could be seen sitting on the fence "with tears in their eyes." A man might observe that conditions appeared to be improving because he just "saw a jackrabbit go by and nobody was chasing it."

And if the moment demanded something more formal, there were always a few lines of mystifying verse that could be used to lend significance to an occasion:

Of all the animals in the barn I'd sooner be a boar.
With every jig he makes a pig and sometimes three or four.

Out in the henhouse, down on my knees
I thought I heard a chicken sneeze.
It was only the rooster saying his prayers
And making love to the hens upstairs.

The Gift Horse

When I was twelve years old my mother bought me a little bay gelding named Tony. I zipped up and down the sideroads every summer for the next five years on that horse, to the various jobs I held on the neighbouring farms. He was as good as owning a car—better, considering that he started every morning and ran on grass. He loved to run and jump, and I shudder to think of the risks I took, riding bareback through the fields with nothing but a halter rope to guide him.

This was in the back of my mind when my twelve-year-old daughter, Maddie, announced that her classmate, Hillary, had run out of pasture options for her seventeen-year-old Appaloosa mare. We were all that stood between poor Zoey and the glue factory.

"There's no such thing as a free horse," I said. "They eat twenty dollar bills." Maddie and her mother waved away my objections, and Zoey arrived about a week later. I put her in the paddock behind the house and went back to my desk, muttering. About fifteen minutes later she jumped the fence and loped off up the road to my neighbour Hughie's farm.

I caught up with her and apologized to Hughie for disrupting his day. He just laughed and patted Zoey on the nose. "You got

Maddie a horse. That's nice. Every little girl wants a horse. That's a nice-looking horse."

I led Zoey back down the road and put her in the barnyard while I strung a piece of electric wire around the paddock. Zoey stayed put for a few days until Maddie and Hillary decided to take her for a walk. Then she slipped through a gate and went cantering off up the road again into Hughie's alfalfa. When I caught up to her, Hughie was standing beside her with a big grin on his face. I apologized once more, explaining that the kids had let her out.

He nodded. "That sounds right." He has five kids of his own, all grown up now.

Zoey put her head down between her knees and coughed a great, rasping, croupy cough that came from her back heels. On the third cough she passed wind with a clap like thunder. Her head came up and she staggered a little to one side.

"I think she has the heaves," I said.

"I believe you're right," said Hughie and he started to chuckle. "But that's good."

"Why is it good?"

"Because if she bolts on Maddie, she's only going to go a hundred yards or so before she has to stop and have a good cough like that. Then Maddie can get off."

"The vet says he can cure the heaves."

"Oh, don't ever do that. You've got the safest horse in the country, right there. Now let me see you ride her home."

Hughie boosted me up and Zoey trotted home through the hayfield, guided with only the rope on her halter. She had a lovely smooth gait, what my old riding master used to call a "gathered trot." With her ears forward and her chin tucked into her chest she made a pretty picture. She stopped twice to cough and appeared much relieved when she reached the barnyard.

The vet gave Zoey the same medication that I use for my asthma. She now has enough zip to give all the kids a couple of laps around the paddock and take me out for a gentle jog in the cool of the evening, up through the fragrant hayfields of the Niagara Escarpment. It's a pleasant reminder of the days when I was young and easy under the apple boughs, and we move slowly enough now that I can appreciate the scenery. When I feel Zoey starting to seize up, I jump off, plug one of her nostrils and give her a couple of puffs of Ventolin. Then I take a puff myself and we walk back to the barn together.

Grandma's Christmas

I have just finished reading an article in one of the daily papers proclaiming the death of the large turkey or ham as a focal point for high holidays. According to the writer, people no longer flock together in great numbers to Grandma's house for high holidays. The new reality for most Canadians is a small gathering in an intimate setting, and the writer suggests a modern menu that offers the "feel" of the holiday without all the drudgery in the kitchen: Cornish hen, quenelles of goat cheese with olive toast points, squash brûlée.

"Hmmph," says my wife. "Christmas in a can." There will be no takers for such a pallid substitute in her family. She was raised on a four-hundred-acre farm in the sandhills of Dufferin County, in southern Ontario, one of six children who shared the same bedroom in a tiny frame house on the edge of the Boyne River Valley. They stuck together like a bunch of bananas, for warmth, for comfort, for encouragement and for entertainment, and this Christmas they will all make the pilgrimage back to the kitchen on the farm for Grandma's forty-fifth Christmas dinner.

Grandma's Christmas was moved to Boxing Day about five years ago, in deference to the full-fledged Christmas celebrations now operated by her offspring. We usually arrive by ten o'clock in the morning and Grandma meets us on the doorstep. She has a large, bright, new kitchen at the farmhouse, about four times the size of the original, which allows the dinner table to be stretched out and set for twenty-four aunts, uncles, cousins and guests. There is always space at Grandma's table for "extras," the single moms, the new immigrants, the dispersed and the dispossessed, all in flight from the sodium glare of the city and the twenty-first century's concept of a Christmas without people. There's still room for a large spruce tree, piles of presents and a wide, circular track around the perimeter to host the invitational speedway races for nineteen grandchildren.

Yes, it is pandemonium. I once asked Grandma, after a particularly boisterous whipped cream fight, if there was any activity she did not allow in her kitchen. She thought for a long moment and said she didn't care for it when the boys drilled deer horn on the table.

The wood stove is going full tilt, and the windows are steamed up from a turkey the size of a Buick roasting in her industrial convection oven. Father trudges up from the barn with a cardboard box containing two baby goats and places it behind the wood stove.

The smells of Christmas are distinct and pungent: turkey and cranberries, fresh-baked buns, turnips and Jello salads, creamed onions and navy beans. Barn boots steaming by the door bring in the smell of cows and horses. Even the snow dusted off coats has a crisp, minty fragrance. After a meal that would fell the average resident of the Third World, the desserts are set out: pies, cakes, trifle, steamed pudding, shortbread cookies and, of course, Grandma's famous butter tarts, or "hand grenades," as I call them, because they tend to go off in my stomach at three in the morning.

Finally chairs are pushed back and the dishes are cleared off the table and replaced by a crokinole board. The stories begin, stories we've all heard before but want to hear again. Father dusts off his accordion and a couple of guitars appear. Before long the women are whooping, the men are singing, the baby goats and the children are whizzing around the room like a banked track and the temperature has risen to eighty-six degrees Fahrenheit.

At this point I have usually had enough and take a walk back through the corn stubble in the still of the evening to cool off and give thanks that, in one place at least, an old-fashioned country Christmas is alive and kicking.

Duke and the Duck

It's a matter of pride that we rarely buy an animal for the farm. Most of the population here is made up of drop-offs, misfits, redundancies and retirees from other households.

Last November a lady gave us a dilapidated mallard drake that had lost his mate to foul play in Wasaga Beach. He looked extremely depressed, so I gave him a spot in the stable with Duke, our "borderline" collie, another refugee with a hard luck story.

For a couple of months the duck stayed under a bench and barely nibbled at the cracked corn I set out for him. He was very withdrawn, and I didn't expect him to last the winter. In January he emerged tentatively from his hiding place, sampled some of the corn and padded around the stable, quacking quietly to himself. I invited him outside to splash in the pond, which was still not frozen, but he declined. He did show a spark of interest in the evening when I brought the dog in for the night. He stood up and quacked until Duke settled down in the straw, and then he moved out into the middle of the floor halfway between the dog's bed and his own. Each night the duck moved a little closer, and by March he was sleeping in Duke's bed. My wife was delighted to see the duck re-entering the world and decided to call him Ferdinand.

Duke was not thrilled about any of this. For starters, he would rather not be seen with a duck. But he resigned himself to the situation with a deeply furrowed brow and a long, mournful sigh.

Duke is an underachiever. He would like to be a sheepdog but he lacks authority. He's never bitten anything in his life and the sheep are catching on. There's one old black-faced ewe that knows Duke's teeth don't meet, and she lingers in the doorway when I put them to bed at night. Duke throws himself at her rump making horrible, throaty, Hound of the Baskervilles noises, but she just stands there and ignores him. Finally, when he's worn himself out and her hind legs are covered with dog slobber, she looks over her shoulder and says, "I'm going in now but not because you told me to."

One morning in the spring, when the breeze was warm and the buds were beginning to break, the duck followed Duke out of the barn, standing at his shoulder and quacking with great enthusiasm in the sunshine. Apart from a short dip in the pond Ferdinand stayed at Duke's shoulder for the rest of the day.

This was too much for Duke. He looked at me and said, "I can't stand it. He talks all the time. All day and all night, it's just quack, quack, quack about nothing. All winter it was, Quack, quack, there's snow on the ground. Quack, quack, we had snow yesterday too. Quack, quack, you sure get a lot of snow around here. Quack, quack, sure is cold, but it's a dry cold . . ."

Two wild mallards landed on our pond the next day, and I watched from the kitchen window as Ferdinand waddled down to join them. If he made some friends, perhaps Duke would get some relief. "C'mon in!" said the wild ducks. "The water's fine!" But Ferdinand just stood on the bank and announced, "This is a private pond. You're welcome to visit if you like, but please don't leave any garbage. We close at sundown."

Then he waddled back up to the barn to find Duke. The wild ducks looked at each other, agreed that Ferdinand was a bit of an odd duck and flew away.

Ferdinand is putting on weight and his plumage has a lovely healthy sheen to it. My wife got some geese to keep him company, but he prefers the company of the dogs. He hangs around the house all day, sleeps in the flowerbeds, quacks at incoming cars, chases cats and looks for a chance to come in and sit on the chesterfield.

I tell guests not to be afraid of the duck. Even the dog will tell you his quack is a lot worse than his bite.

Hannah and the Chicks

The day started out peacefully enough. The three older kids caught the school bus in time. I fed the animals, and my wife drove off to a physio appointment for her sprained ankle. I was just sitting down to a cup of coffee when I realized that Hannah, the four-year-old, had disappeared.

This happens a lot. She's a very single-minded child, a thinker with a strong sense of purpose. When she goes missing, you know she hasn't just wandered off. She's on a mission.

I checked the house, the road, the pond, the garden, jogged around the barn and found nothing. At the nine-minute mark my spinal muscles were going into spasm and I forced myself to stop and think. Then I noticed the dogs were gone too. Wherever Hannah goes, the dogs follow. On a hunch, I went into the office and looked in the box of chicks we had just incubated. Last night, there were six and now there were five.

"All right," I said to myself. "She's taken a chick and gone off with the dogs. She's outside someplace and she's not answering me because she knows she's not supposed to touch the chicks."

I finally found her out in the orchard in her red raincoat and boots, with a shovel, digging a hole under one of the apple trees. A satin-lined jewellery box from her mother's bedside table lay on the ground beside her. I knelt down, opened the box and found the chick lying in state with flowers and feathers arranged carefully around it. It looked like Snow White. The four dogs and the duck sat in a row beside her, like Doc, Grumpy, Happy, Sleepy and Bashful.

I caught my breath and sat down beside her. "Hannah," I said, "I promise I won't be cross with you. But I want you to tell me what happened to this chick."

She turned up her face and two big tears rolled down her cheeks. "I gave it a drink and it died!" she wailed.

"Oh dear," I said. "That's why you're not supposed to pick them up."

She pulled the corner of her mouth down in an agony of self-recrimination. "I just gave him a drink and then he put his head back and he died."

We buried the chick, and I answered her questions about life after death as best I could. Then we went for a walk. Like the thoughts of most people after a funeral, hers quickly turned to food.

"Can I get the eggs?" she asked.

She scampered into the henhouse and emerged with an egg in each hand.

"Eggs on toast, Daddy!" she shouted and dashed off to the house. She ran about fifteen feet, stumbled and fell and smashed one of the eggs. Frustrated, she got to her feet, took the other egg and threw it at the side of the truck.

When people ask us why we live in the country, we babble about peace and quiet, growing your own vegetables and watching sunsets. But it's really something much more subtle than any of that. A friend of mine once put his finger on it for me when he said that country life offers "moments of clarity" that aren't as easy to come by anywhere else.

As Hannah trudged off to the house muttering about the broken eggs, I could see several of her female relatives marching along beside her. Like them, she has great inventiveness, infinite tenderness, bone-headed determination, and a capacity for fits and furies that should strike terror in the hearts of men everywhere.

When I got back to the house, Hannah was missing again. This time I found her sitting on the office chair with the five chicks under her skirt. "I'm keeping them warm," she said. "I'm their mother and I think I'll lay another egg."

Burglars in the Barn

When Michel de Montaigne retired from government service in 1571 and moved out to the countryside in France to write the essays that would make him famous to later generations, his friends were very worried. Private armies roamed the land, and the countryside was a very dangerous place to be unless you lived in a fortified house.

Montaigne waved away their concerns. The secret, he said, was to live in a way that made it clear you had nothing worth plundering. "Unless you are well-fortified, it is best not to be fortified at all." He lived undisturbed in his family estate for the next twenty years.

Out here on the Ninth Concession I have tried to live by Montaigne's dictum. Burglars are at work almost every week along the top of the hill in the big houses and the ski chalets. Break-ins and car thefts are so common that the police seldom come out to visit the scene anymore. They just take the details by phone and tell you to call your insurance company. One retired gentleman of my acquaintance, whose liquor cabinet, stereo system and TV had been removed by thieves in the night, had the temerity to insist on a house call by the police. The officers noticed a little .22 rifle leaning up against the wall that the man used for shooting squirrels off his birdfeeder and wanted to charge him with improper storage of a firearm. He threw them out.

Last week we heard a truck backing up the lane to the barn at four o'clock in the morning and my wife sent me out to investigate. By the time I fumbled around and found my socks, the truck drove off and we feared the worst. I jogged out to the barn and turned on the lights. The doors were wide open, but nothing was missing. We had been inspected and passed over.

Montaigne would have approved, but the experience left me feeling . . . well, violated. I have collected all this stuff with care over twenty-five years and it is precious to me. People I didn't even know had dismissed it all as worthless.

A friend in the insurance business tells me that cash, jewellery and electronics are the first choice of thieves. He says that if they have a choice between a Rolex watch and a 1948 Massey seven-foot hay mower that weighs five hundred pounds and needs sharpening, they are more likely to take the watch. Certain vehicle models are regular targets, but my 1983 Ford pickup with the cow cartoons painted on the racks isn't on the list. We hear reports of rustling in the county, but rustlers are looking for animals in their prime, not a milk goat in her teens who plants all four feet in the dirt when you try to lead her somewhere.

I was burgled once in 1978, when I was restoring the old frame house on the farm with one power tool, a very eccentric seven-and-a-quarter-inch circular saw. I left the saw out on the veranda one weekend and someone swiped it. I am much indebted to that thief because he freed me from the tyranny of that awful saw. By stealing it from me he forced me to go out and buy a decent one.

I suppose someone could make off with my truck, but they would have to know in advance that you have to squirt gas into the carburetor before it will start. The gas squirter is on the bench in the middle barn where the gander sleeps, and the gander bites everyone but me. And then you would have to pull the manure spreader out of the way before you could back the truck out of the lane. There's a yellow jacket nest hanging off the tongue of the spreader, not the sort of thing you would want to bump into in the middle of the night. So if you are thinking of taking my truck, it might be safer to give me a call first the way the neighbours do.

Good and Perfect Gifts

At the end of the year, when the sunflowers bow their heads to the ground and the frost glistens on the rail fences, I find myself reflecting on the past growing season, which invariably starts with great promise and then stumbles in mid-season and limps to the finish line.

After a balmy and moist June, a severe drought brought our garden to a standstill and dried up the pastures. By August I was feeding hay and watering the stock out of the well, which is always a dicey business. I carried pails of water from the pond until it was a puddle of moist clay and so managed to keep the tomatoes and some young apple trees going. But the potatoes were like marbles, and the beans and peas shrivelled back into the dust. The rains finally came but too late to make much difference.

At the fall fair I visited the sheep barn and passed pen after pen of giant lambs that made mine look like rabbits. I wondered if they might be from out of province, but the certificates stapled to the stalls said they were from my own township. Our beef heifer, on which I had placed such high hopes (and about three tons of grain corn), dragged my son around the 4-H ring like a powerboat with a water skier. She placed third in a class of three.

I did win a prize for a duck this year. I put Ferdinand in the waterfowl class for Best Rouen Drake and was pleasantly surprised to find a red ribbon on his cage. But then I made the mistake of discussing my triumph with the Poultry Committee. The judge told me that although Ferdinand was better than the other two ducks in the class, he still wasn't much of a duck. Taking out his Poultry Standards bible that he carries with him, the judge showed me the proper shape of a Rouen drake, sort of like a Viking ship, with a nice flat keel. Ferdinand is shaped more like a teapot. "He's a nice colour, though," said the judge.

I'm not sure what I expected. Ferdinand was a gift, after all, like most of the animals we own. We have Zoey the gift horse, who, because of her breathing difficulties, stands all day under the apple tree swatting flies. The sheep themselves were a gift (part of my wife's dowry), and if you tied me up and tortured me with a hot poker, I still couldn't tell you what breed they are. Even our first sheepdog, Bobbie, was a gift, and she was terrified of the sheep.

It was with all this in mind that I leaned on the truck box with my dairy farmer neighbour and contemplated the sorry state of the farm after a tough season. "This is the moment for which stock trucks were invented," he said. "You can always clear the place out and make a new start."

My wife says perhaps not. Since we do not rely on any of this for a living, there is no reason to look for either profits or prize ribbons. She has the wisdom to see all of it as a gift. She will be content to remember the 2001 fall fair as the year that the two other kids in the 4-H beef class both handed their halter ropes to our son and offered to trade calves with him. She will pin up the photo of our four-year-old, wearing a hockey helmet and butting heads on the front lawn with her pet goat, Finky. And she'll laugh about the day the pigs escaped, gleefully snooted up the orchard and romped up to the front veranda carrying one of the young apple trees I'd been pouring water on all summer.

And that will be reason enough to do it all over again.

Mental Health Day in the City

When my wife and I decided to leave the city fourteen years ago, our friends divided up into two groups. Half of them told us we were crazy and the other half asked, "Can we come too?"

We shared their feelings. My wife grew up in the country, and she still loves to make our children's eyes grow wide with stories of rescue missions to feed cattle trapped by heavy snow and smashing through ice with an axe to water horses. When they complain they're bored, she reminds them that she and her little sister used to play with pebbles and sticks all day long in a fence corner while her father plowed the field.

But one year in an apartment in downtown Toronto the first year we were married gave her a taste for smoked salmon on a bagel and certain coffee concoctions that cannot be ordered in a single declarative sentence. She discovered Thai food, curry houses, art galleries, foreign films, American magazines and kitchen stores.

We still agree the farm is the best place to raise our family, but there are moments when we miss the city. Sometimes on a mid-winter night I have watched out my window as streams of snow blow through the bare apple trees and jackrabbits chase one another in mad circles in the moonlight. I wonder if human beings were really supposed to live in Nottawasaga Township all year round. You can't find *The New Yorker* on the magazine rack in the drug store in our hometown, and there has never been a film with subtitles at the Gayety Theatre. We both know the menu for the Swiss Chalet and the village diner off by heart.

There's nothing we like better in mid-February than hurtling south on the freeway late on a Friday afternoon to a downtown hotel. We zip along in the southbound lane, passing miles of traffic crawling its way out of the city, and we follow our old route down Avenue Road past our old apartment to the Park Plaza. I toss the keys to the doorman and dispatch the luggage to the room while my wife goes foraging for fruits and cheeses and some sensational reading. I find a handful of freesias for the room from the flower shop next door and buy a stack of American political magazines. Saturday morning finds us lounging in terrycloth robes with the weekend papers piled around us, rediscovering the joy of a completed sentence.

A lovely picture, but it's getting harder and harder to pull it off. The neighbour who used to do chores for us celebrated his seventy-ninth birthday by moving into town last fall. The three dogs have to go up the hill to a doggie bed and breakfast. I have to fill up the round bale feeders for the cows and the horse and rig up a frost-free automatic watering system. The rabbits need a two-day supply of carrots, and I pour out a pile of corn on the barn floor for the guinea hens.

The children are now getting past the age when we can drop them at Grandma's farm for the weekend without loud protests, for they too have heard the siren call of the city. They want to see all their aunts and uncles and godmothers and godfathers. They have to play their annual game of Super Mario on the hotel TV and order room service. They talk to people in elevators, run up and down corridors in their bare feet and explain their brother's jokes to the next table in the restaurant. My wife and I plod after them like two tired shepherds, moving from pool to museum to mall, and then return home exhausted.

Clearly we have to rethink the whole exercise. I am pleased to report that we have found a childless couple who need a getaway in the country away from their downtown condo, and they think we have really nice kids.

Life and Character

O ne of the reasons I enjoy living in the country is that here you still find people who make their livings from three or four occupations rather than one. My wife and I run two home businesses, keep a small farm, raise four kids and do volunteer work in the community. We wake up in the morning surrounded by things that must be done and move through the day with no clear line separating work from the rest of our lives.

This is an old model for living and, although chaotic at times, it has suited us well for the last fifteen years. There is no commute, no meetings, no staff and no boss. We have more in common with a farm family from fifty years ago than we do with many of our friends. Getting to this point was no accident. We both gave considerable thought to this way of living, using examples from our past.

One summer while I was at university, I took a job picking pears in the south of France for Monsieur and Madame Pilat, a couple who farmed a small orchard on the Durance River in Provence. He was a rotund fellow in his mid-fifties with a Maurice Chevalier smile and a wide straw hat. She was younger, darkly beautiful and serene, with a deeply tanned face and laugh lines around her eyes.

We rose when it was still dark to pick figs and returned to the pink stucco farmhouse at dawn for a breakfast on the patio. After breakfast we went to the pear orchard and picked until noon, and then we sat down to the big meal of the day. We had a siesta after lunch, went back to the orchard in mid-afternoon and came in at dark for a light supper. This went on six days a week for two weeks.

One day I asked Monsieur Pilat if I could go into town to buy a part for my bicycle. "But of course, *mon brave!*" he said. "If you have something to do, off you go. We'll leave some pears for you for when you get back."

I couldn't be sure if he was making fun of my work ethic. But when I returned, he apologized, telling me that he had to make an effort to remember that not everyone was as thrilled about picking pears as he was. He loved everything about the land under his feet. Like everyone in Provence, he was a gourmand and would talk all morning about *les andouillettes*—the sausages we were having for lunch—and how he'd gathered the rosemary and the anise to spice them. He would list the vegetables he had grown for the summer pistou, the aroma of which wafted through the orchard from the kitchen. He would caution us not to step on the golf-ball-sized snails that moved in the grass below the pear trees. Then he would pluck a perfectly formed Anjou pear and exclaim, "*La belle poire!*" as if it were the first one he had ever seen.

Work was his life and life was his work, and it struck me at the tender age of nineteen that this was a very good way to live. On my last night at the farm we had a boisterous discussion about farm economics over a bottle of red wine and a feast of escargots we had gathered. I remember him leaning forward and poking me in the chest with his stubby finger.

"*Et vous, monsieur l'economiste,*" he said solemnly. "When you are prime minister, you must remember me, *le paysan.*"

It is now thirty years later, and I am a long way from being prime minister. But I do remember Monsieur Pilat, and I think he would be pleased to know that I found my way to this place.

Humpty Dumpty

I 've found it isn't a good idea to make my animals the subject of literature or art. It seems that as soon as they have their portraits done or if I mention them in my writing, they die. It is with great sadness that I must report the passing of both Duke the dog and Ferdinand the duck.

A car bumped Duke when he was just a year old, and he sustained a back injury that resulted in a permanent debilitating spinal disorder that made life very difficult for him. When he reached the age of eight, we knew we would have to put him to sleep. We prepared Ferdinand for this sad event as best we could and located a mate for him at the fall fair, a quiet little mottled duck that Hannah named Felicity Roseanna, in honour of her favourite member of the fair board. Felicity was a show duck and Ferdinand was delighted with her, but he couldn't make up his mind about sleeping arrangements, because he was very used to making a nest of Duke's tummy and paws at night. Felicity was graceful about his indecision until the evening of Duke's last day, when his straw pile in the stable remained empty. I came out next morning and found Felicity sitting by herself on the straw pile, looking pretty much disgusted. Ferdinand had slipped through the rungs of the feeder during the night into the sheep pen and was nestled beside a fluffy old ewe.

This went on for several months. I knew this was risky behaviour for a duck, but I did nothing to discourage it. A sheep is not careful about when and where it decides to flop down for the night and, once down, is deaf to all suggestions about getting up. Sure enough, one morning in June as the old sheep struggled to her feet, I found poor Ferdinand pressed flat into the straw and very stiff.

Hannah was heartbroken. She sat for a long time on the garden wall cradling Ferdinand in her arms, tears rolling down her cheeks, begging him to wake up again. We buried him beside Duke under a carpet of pink blossoms from the crab-apple tree in a moving ceremony the whole family attended, and we planted crocus bulbs over him. A few weeks later, we found a mail-order husband for Felicity, and life in the stable returned to normal.

In the dentist office the other day, Hannah handed me one of those New Age children's books out of Kansas City that celebrate uplifting examples of sharing and goodness. This one had revisited the story of Humpty Dumpty to give it a happy ending, showing how all the king's horses and all the king's men used teamwork, cooperation and a bit of Krazy Glue to solve a problem.

This story failed to impress Hannah, because at five she already knows that when eggs break, there's nothing you can do about it. Stuff happens. The world changes and you have to gather yourself up and go on. Sometimes you just can't put Humpty Dumpty back together again.

That's an important lesson, and although it's painful to watch as a five-year-old learns it, I wouldn't shield her from it. This is just one of the gifts that flow from a life on the land surrounded by animals and family and neighbours. There are more lessons to come, I'm sure.

Her mother and I just hope that she will profit from Ferdinand's example and learn sometime before her sixteenth birthday just how perilous it is to date outside your species.

Family Reunion

O ne Sunday afternoon last June we drove the kids about an hour west of us to a farm in the heart of Grey County for the forty-sixth annual reunion of my wife's mother's family.

This year it took place at the farm of Ed and Velda Jack, a warm and friendly couple who are the fifth generation of Jacks to work the marshy soils of Proton Township.

As reunions go, it was a lot of fun. Ed roasted one of his pigs, Velda's kitchen tables sagged under the weight of salads, pickles, pies, cakes and jugs of lemonade. After the kids soaked themselves tossing water balloons and snatched up handfuls of Tootsie Rolls in the candy toss, they flew kites, played baseball and circled the house at a gallop dousing one another with supersoakers and pails of water. Over the din the elders visited and told stories . . . wonderful stories.

William and Euphemia Jack left Forfarshire, Scotland, in the spring of 1854 with nine children and sailed to Canada, arriving in Hamilton, Ontario, in the late summer, where their tenth child, Ainsworth, was born. From there, they travelled fifty miles north to Shingle's Shanty, Egremont, which was at that time a settlement on the edge of the virgin forests of Grey County. The Jacks chopped a path for their two oxen and wagon through the last twelve miles of dense bush to reach their four hundred acres on Lot 15, Ninth Concession, Proton.

The family spent the first winter in a hastily constructed log shanty, living on a supply of potatoes and turnips they had carried in. They were forced to slaughter one of the oxen to tide them over to spring. In May, Euphemia was struck with a virulent fever and died. Grief-stricken but resolute, William did not abandon the enterprise. He conducted a funeral service, buried his wife in the woods near the shanty and made the journey back to Egremont to buy a horse.

My wife's great-great-grandfather, Charles Jack, was about ten years old that spring when his father put an axe in his hands and sent him into the forest with his other brothers to begin clearing the trees. He always remembered his father plowing around the stumps the second season with the ox and the horse harnessed together. He also remembered the runaway slave who stayed with them on his journey from a Georgia plantation to freedom.

One of the Jack brothers later wrote that Proton Township was one of the "most damnable places in the world," overgrown with "adder tongue, cow cabbage, leeks and ground hemlock to no end," and the land under water six months of the year. Killing frosts ruined the first crops. "The cows ate better than we did," he declared. They survived the following winter on biscuits made from frozen potatoes and flour.

Several years later William moved Euphemia's remains to the cemetery of the new Esplin church, just west of the farm, where hers was the first burial. As the years went by, most of the Jack boys went off to fight in the American Civil War, saying they would rather be shot at than spend another year on that wretched farm. Only two boys remained. Charles moved to his own farm a mile away and Ainsworth, the baby, took over the home farm. Their older sister, Jean Jack, married Alexander McPhail and moved to his farm on the Twelfth Concession. Their granddaughter, Agnes, became the first woman elected to the House of Commons in Canada.

In 1911, fifty-six years after he arrived in Proton, Charles and his wife, Catherine, posed for a photograph on the veranda of their new brick house with all twenty-four grandchildren. Catherine is seated, holding the youngest child on her lap. The baby is Katie Jack, my wife's grandmother, now ninety years old and the last living member of that happy picnic scene.

I found it fascinating to watch my son look at the photograph and make the connection between his great-grandmother, the baby in arms and the tired face of the pioneer woman. I explained to him that Granny Kate knew people who crossed the Atlantic in tall ships and cleared the trees from this farm. He looked at the photo, at Granny Kate sitting in a lawn chair and at Ed and Velda's veranda.

"Could we take another picture like this, with everybody in it?" he asked.

"Yes, of course," I said. And we did just that.

Retirement, Equine Style

Our old horse has a birthday coming up and we're wondering how to celebrate.

When my neighbour Tim Armour delivered Zoey to us three years ago, I asked how old she was. Now, horse people never give you the real age of a horse if they can possibly help it. That's a given. And because horses live so long and get passed around so much, by the time they're on their fifth owner, even an honest person like Tim can be out by three or four years.

"About eighteen or nineteen," he said. Not bad, I thought, assuming that she was probably closer to twenty-one. There would still be a few good years left in her. But Zoey's cough made it difficult to ride her. I indulged her with expensive herbal preparations, feed treatments, hay cubes, about two bags of carrots a week and a special sweet feed that costs more than granola.

My father-in-law, who has worked with horses all his life, took one look at Zoey and winced. "Jeez," he said, "not an Appaloosa!"

"Is that bad?" I asked.

"Well, you know why the Sioux rode Appaloosas to Little Bighorn, don't you?"

I confessed that I didn't.

"So they'd be good and mad when they got there."

I quickly discovered why Zoey wore out her welcome. She was a fence buster and explorer. There were several escapes over the next six months, all ending peacefully in the same hayfield at the back of the farm. Then, one morning in late winter, she climbed up on a rotten snowbank and jumped over a gate to go for one of her little frolics. She climbed over the same snow bank to get back in, and it collapsed under her. When I found her, she was caught in the gate, upside down in a mudhole with a terrible gash in her leg. More vet bills and tender care eventually restored her to health.

The girls soon lost interest in Zoey, but my youngest, Hannah, eventually took riding lessons down in Creemore. Robert, her instructor, took me aside one day and said he wanted me to meet someone. He introduced me to a frail old lady leaning on a cane and explained that she had been Zoey's original owner.

"Then you'll be able to tell me how old she is," I said.

"Yes," she said. "I foaled her out in the spring of 1971."

"Good heavens," I exclaimed. "That means she's thirty-two years old!"

This horse remembers Richard Nixon as a popular president. They still had a passenger train to Flesherton. Gas was fifty cents a gallon.

Zoey has finally learned to accept the convention of a fence. I'm making a granny flat box stall for her for stormy nights, even though my father-in-law says she is better off living outside. She stands in the pasture next to the house all day with her eyes half closed, beside a goat born in 1989 and a tractor made in 1953. Visitors always stop to give her a carrot out of the bucket and a pat, so she has lots of company. And the neighbours now give directions using her as a signpost. "You go about a half-mile from the highway and when you see a really old horse, you turn left."

The School Trip

As the snow retreats to the fencerows and the buds begin to swell, I prepare to greet my least favourite time of the year— the season of the school trip.

In my day, at Allenby Public School in North Toronto in 1959, there was no such thing as a school trip. We didn't go overnight to the conservation area or on a bus to a pioneer village or on a hockey trip to Japan. Nowadays the kids hardly ever see the inside of a classroom. Between school trips, strikes, ice storms, fevers and suspensions, my four kids are home three days out of five.

My grade four teacher, Miss Brown, was an innovator, and she thought we should all get out and visit a farm. There was a kid in the class whose father ran a chicken farm north of the city. I think Miss Brown had the idea that this would be a little barnyard with a haystack in it and a bunch of brown hens scratching up the dirt. It turned out to be a chicken factory, and they wouldn't allow us in the barn to see the live chickens because they were worried about spreading disease to the flock. But they did take us through the plant where we saw the chickens get tied upside down to a track, zoom along and get zapped by an electric needle, then dunked in a hot water tank and plucked by a big rubber machine that slapped all the feathers off.

My seatmate on the bus, Robbie, didn't have the faintest idea where chicken came from and he took one look at this scene and threw up on the floor. We were all quickly herded back onto the bus. Robbie threw up all the way home; in fact, all you had to do after that was cluck like a chicken and you could make Robbie throw up.

That was it for the school trips for quite a while. Miss Brown had a date in front of the school board and was reprimanded for upsetting the children and we went back to field days and school plays for our entertainment.

But that little outing had an enormous effect on me. Within a few months I was keeping chickens myself, at the family farm near Alliston where my mother, who was a writer, moved us every spring to escape from the city. She built a little barn for her Jersey cow, with pens for other animals as well. My brother and I bought a hundred chicks from the local feed store and put them under a lamp. We fed and watered them all summer, dressed them in the fall and when we got back to the city for the winter, we ran around the neighbourhood selling frozen chicken to all our friends. At Christmas, my mother totted up the results and gave each of us a crisp, new five-dollar bill.

Mother had hoped this would be a learning experience that would encourage us in the knowledge that hard work and thrift would inevitably lead to success. But it had the opposite effect on my brother. I will always remember him staring at that five-dollar bill, knowing this was all he was ever going to see out of that summer's work, and I could see that the experience had embittered him for life. He never got over that early disappointment with the chickens. The poor man ended up teaching high school English.

A sad story. As for me, getting all my expenses back plus five dollars was all the encouragement I needed to do it all over again. Even then you could see that I had the makings of a farmer.

This week my kids are off to the four points of the compass, one to see the sights of Niagara Falls, another to examine the effects of global warming in the Minesing Wetlands (aka The Swamp). Who knows, one of them may have an experience that will change their life, as I did.

Community Spirit

The community hall in the little village of Duntroon, just around the corner from us, has an interesting story. It was originally an army barracks from nearby Canadian Forces Base Borden, declared surplus by the military in 1952 and offered to the village for six hundred dollars. The lot was created through the generosity of Jack and Mary Swalm, who ran a local service station. Jack offered thirty feet off the back of his property and the Women's Institute sliced ten feet off their baseball park on the other side. The concept of a "setback" had not been invented in Duntroon at that time.

"They needed forty feet and that's exactly what they got," says Jack, who is now ninety-two. "Imagine trying something like that today. Well, you couldn't do it and you'd still need a room full of lawyers and planners to tell you it couldn't be done."

A crew of young volunteers went down to the base, took the barracks apart piece by piece, brought it up on trucks and reassembled it on a new foundation. A train from Toronto delivered a donation of steel beams and cement to the station east of the village. It was all loaded onto wagons and freighted up to the site with teams of horses. By the time the steel beams and cement were in place, the only expense the committee incurred was about six dollars for welding rods.

"It's a poor job that can't afford a boss," says Jack. But in fact, there was no boss for the assembly of the hall. Over that summer and the next year, hundreds of volunteers worked on the building. On wet days when the farmers couldn't work the fields, they'd bring their tools and spend hours on it. The committee wanted the hall to be on the cutting edge of entertainment, so they put a bowling alley in the basement early in 1955. By that time the volunteer effort was finally running out of steam, and the committee broke down and hired two carpenters to finish the job of installing cupboards in the kitchen.

The grand opening was held on June 30, 1955. The Evans family orchestra provided music. A man named F.A. Lashley came up from the Ministry of Agriculture to clip the ribbon and speak. The Ag Rep, Keith McKruer, spoke, as did MPP Rev. Wally Downer and about nine other dignitaries. A flag was presented by the Glen Huron Orange Lodge. Greetings were brought from the National Farm Radio Forum, from the warden of Simcoe County and from the chairman of the Hall Committee. Between each speech was a bit of music, including a duet by young Grant Sampson and Judy McNichol, a tap dance by Douglas Walker and another duet by Gordon and Bob Holt. The evening finished with dancing to the Evans orchestra on the freshly sanded floor. A good time was had by all.

Since that time the hall has been the site of countless dances, wedding receptions, anniversaries, reunions, all-candidates meetings, landfill site protests, retirements, 4-H Club meetings and, of course, bowling tournaments. One thing I've always liked about this hall is that no matter how hot the protest meeting gets, you can always hear the rumble of a bowling ball rolling in the basement. It's a calming sound and somehow comforting to be reminded that at least four people in the township don't give a rip about what's happening upstairs.

"It was a real community project," remembers Jack. "I don't suppose you could do it today."

But then I reminded him of two recent church projects that were built just the same way and we agreed that, of course, you could. And if we ever seriously doubt our potential, all we have to do is look at that little white building on the hill in Duntroon and remember what a group of like-minded people can accomplish for a good cause.

An Anniversary

Twenty-five years ago, on June 1, 1978, I formally took possession of an abandoned farmstead on a dead-end road in the Pretty River Valley southwest of Collingwood, Ontario.

There were a number of things I liked about my little farm. The land was heavy clay but tile drained and still in crop. It had a few acres of hardwood bush at the back, and a little creek meandered through a gully behind the barn and house. The buildings were in rough shape, but someone had taken the trouble to put a new roof on the house within living memory and the inside was still sound. A little grove of ancient apple and pear trees stood in the front yard. In the still of that spring morning tractors hummed in the surrounding fields and mist rose off the freshly turned earth.

I knew then that this place would make a good home. For the next ten years I was a weekender, but I made friends with the neighbours. By night I warmed to their wood stoves and the easy hospitality of Arborite kitchen tables. By day the air was filled with the ear-stopping sounds and the nose-stopping smells of working farms.

Each summer I took my holidays in a lump to attack some major project. I planted trees, carved out a garden, performed chiropractic work on the sagging barn and restored the house. I became a regular attendee at local functions, volunteered for fieldwork in hay season and tried to get everybody together for a barbecue at least once a year. When I got married the neighbours turned out in force to dance at my wedding. Six months later, when my wife discovered she was expecting, we decided that my writing could support us, and we both quit our jobs in the city to become permanent residents here. We built fences and a barn, and stocked the farm with sheep, goats, a horse and a cow. Three more children followed. We were drafted onto the fair board, joined the 4-H Club, and volunteered to help with hospital fundraisers and the community theatre.

On the whole I think we have adapted quite well. We accept that high-speed internet, cable TV and gas pipelines will never reach the Ninth Concession in our lifetime. We struggle each year with cluster flies, soil that turns to concrete in a dry spell, ferocious winters that leave us stranded for days on end and the vague feeling that stuff is happening somewhere and we don't know about it. But we also feel blessed that we are able to work at home with a schedule dictated as much by weather and the season as by any artificial business deadline we might impose on ourselves.

After twenty-five years the neighbourhood has also changed dramatically as the farmers, one by one, retire and move into town. The land is still cultivated, but the machines usually visit for only a few minutes at a time, in the spring and the fall. Even so I still have plenty of company. There are even a few other home-office types like me who have discovered that once you take meetings and commuting out of your day, you have to spend only a couple of hours at the desk to get the same amount of work done. To my surprise some of them share my interest in old machinery and exotic chickens. I miss the old characters who made life so entertaining, but my wife tells me not to worry. There is a whole new crop coming on, and I am probably one of them.

It's only because of some Byzantine astrologer that we mark our days out in decades and quarter-centuries. But there should be a moment, from time to time, when we pause to take stock of the progress in our lives.

On the first of June this year I sat on the porch of the farm-house doing just that.

Will I Ever Be a Local?

I've lived on this farm for twenty-five years now, which I think earns me the right to call myself a local. But my wife, who was born here, thinks I will never qualify. She says that if you come from away, you have to die in bed in the farmhouse before your farm will ever be known as the Old Needles Place.

There's an old story about a woman who was born on the mail boat that sailed from Halifax to St. John's, Newfoundland. She lived in St. John's for a century. When she finally died the newspaper headline read: "Halifax woman dead at 100."

Years ago, I interviewed a hundred-year-old woman in the little village of Hockley for the local newspaper and asked her if she had always lived in this valley. She shook her head sadly and said no, and I raised my pen, ready to record the wanderings that had brought her to this place. She told me she had been born in Mono Centre, all of seven miles away, and came in a horse and buggy to Hockley the day she was married. She died a short time after I interviewed her, and I remember one of her neighbours wondering aloud at the funeral, "Why wouldn't she want to be buried at home in Mono Centre?"

These days, there are so few pure laine country people left on the concession roads that we may be in need of a new category of membership, much as sons and daughters of veterans are now allowed to join the Legion. A few simple questions could be asked, a small fee paid and (assuming that the answers are correct) you could be granted the status of an "almost local."

Here are some of the questions you might be asked:

Do you have just one suit for weddings and funerals? Do you save plastic buckets? Do you leave your car doors unlocked at all times? Do you have an inside dog and an outside dog? Has your outside dog never been to town? When you pass a neighbour in the car, do you wave from the elbow or do you merely raise one finger from the steering wheel? Do you have trouble keeping the car or truck going in a straight line because you are looking at crops and livestock? Do you sometimes find yourself sitting in the car in the middle of a dirt road chatting with a neighbour out the window while other cars take to the ditch to get around you? Can you tell whose tractor is going by without looking out the window? Can people recognize you from three hundred yards away by the way you walk or the tilt of your hat? If somebody honks their horn at you, do you automatically smile and wave? Do most of your conversations open with some observation about the weather? Is your most important news source the store in the village? Have you had surgery in the local hospital? If you hear about a death or a fire in the community, does the woman in your house immediately start making sandwiches or a cake? Do you sometimes find yourself referring to a farm in the neighbourhood by the name of someone who owned it more than twenty-five years ago?

If you answered yes to all of the above questions, consider it official: you are a local. But they'll still call your farm the Old Currie Place.

This reminds me of the story of the Englishman who drops into the clubhouse of the famously exclusive golf course to inquire if he might be allowed to play a round. The steward informs him that the only possibility is if he is invited as a guest of a member. The steward then guides him to a sleepy old codger in a leather chair in the smoking room. The old man opens one eye, hears the gentleman's request and proceeds to grill him about his professional and military background. The gentleman delivers all the correct answers: Eton, Oxford, partnership in an old London law firm, the Guards, MC, DSO and Bar. The old man finally turns to the steward and says, gruffly, "Nine holes."

A Sermon in the Fields

E very summer our little Anglican church holds an outdoor
service and farm picnic generously hosted by a couple in our
congregation. This year I was asked to give the homily. I chose as
my theme the tension that has long existed between Christianity
and environmentalists, who love to take aim at the passage in
Genesis 1:28 in which God, having just given Adam and Eve
"dominion" over the animals and the birds and the fishes, instructs
the couple "to be fruitful and multiply and replenish the earth, and
subdue it."

One of my oldest friends teaches environmental ethics at York
University and is a practising Buddhist. I have been debating spir-
itual matters with Peter for about forty years now. We both like to
hedge our bets, which means I sit beside him while he spins his
prayer wheel and he sometimes slips into our family pew at church
when he comes to visit. Peter points out that most ecologists have
never read any further than verse 28 and so may be forgiven for
not realizing that virtually all the rest of the Bible contradicts their
narrow interpretation of that one passage. The call to stewardship
is everywhere, and that call is often stern and uncompromising.
A seventh of the land must lie fallow each year, and we are not
supposed to reap to the edges of the field or strip the vineyard

bare. Fallen fruit or anything else beyond our needs should be left for the poor.

The concept of stewardship has been amplified in all sorts of literary traditions that flow from the Bible, guiding early naturalists such as Henry David Thoreau, Ralph Waldo Emerson and John Muir. The Mormon writer Hugh Nibley summed it up quite clearly when he wrote, "Man's dominion is a call to service, not a licence to exterminate."

So Peter the Buddhist and Dan the stumbling Anglican have agreed that there is no real clash between the demands of the environmental movement and the demands of scripture. But this is where Peter gets going on me. His criticism of Christians and just about everybody else in the Western world centres on the way we ignore our obvious responsibilities to God's creation. It would be understandable if there were a verse 29 that suggests we leave the allocation of the earth's resources to the free market economy. But there is not.

Instead we find a clear and direct order not to engage in usury. Charging interest on a debt is forbidden because the dispossession and impoverishment of one group of people should never be seen as an economic opportunity for others, for it destroys community. The voice that gave us that stern rule understood that greed upsets the fragile economy of a farm and forces farmers to do self-destructive things, for instance, rely on energy sources not found on the farm, ramp up production and use expensive chemical fertilizers and pesticides. The proof is that all of the family farms that once flourished on the road where we held our church service last summer are now gone, as they are gone from roads across the country.

Most of us, however, including the elders at my very own church, seek the highest available return on our savings account at the local credit union. Even Peter the Buddhist gave my daughter a Canada Savings Bond at her christening, to which we welcomed him as honorary pagan godfather.

I remember chuckling with him about that humdinger on usury while we were munching egg salad sandwiches in the parish hall after the baptism. We agreed ruefully that we were both part of a terribly compromised world. Compromised perhaps—but, as the poet Wendell Berry reminds, us we can still ally ourselves with those things that are worthy: the traditions of good work and responsible thought. We can still care for water, earth, air, plants and animals, families and communities. We can still enjoy stories and songs, the company of neighbours and friends and the sun on our faces as we gather in an open field to count our blessings.

A Sheep Romance

We have been keeping sheep here at the farm for nearly fifteen years now. There is no explanation for it apart from the fact that I like them. Financially they are a lost cause. They are such a drain on the household income that we have come to the conclusion that their numbers must be limited. The rule is: no more than ten ewes in the barn.

Sheep have appeared at several turning points in my life. When I was twelve, the farmer who lived next door to my mother's hobby farm gave us an orphaned lamb to bottle feed, because he couldn't be bothered with it. We called her Myrtle and she grew to be a complete pest, jumping up on visitors like a dog and butting my mother headfirst into her flowerbeds. When I went off to boarding school that fall, Mother announced that Myrtle could go too. The headmaster had agreed that the sheep could live down at the horse stables and be a mascot for the football team.

Maybe she thought turning up on the first day of school with a sheep in the back seat of our Volkswagen Bug would help build character. But it took a year and a half of fist fights before I could walk down a hallway without hearing someone call "Baa!" after me. Myrtle and I both survived the experience, and she lived out her days happily on the farm next door to the school.

After high school I went off to the Australian outback for a year to find myself and eventually landed on a sheep station in western Queensland. At dawn on the first day my employers, Mick and Dave, took me to an enormous truck that had just arrived crammed full of sheep.

"Danny," said Mick. "Climb in there and throw every sheep off that has no top front teeth."

I grabbed a sheep, pulled up its lip and, as luck would have it, found no top front teeth. I pitched it down the chute and grabbed another. Same thing. This went on for about twenty minutes before I called out, "Mick, none of these sheep have any top front teeth."

Mick grinned at Dave and said, "Forty-two. I believe the lad's set a new record."

Then they put me to work "dagging." They would drive me through the scrub until we found a flock of sheep and drop me off with two sheepdogs (also named Mick and Dave) and a pair of hand shears. The dogs would run in circles around the flock, bunching the sheep together so tightly that I could wade into the middle of them and go to work. I was supposed to find the ones with manure caked on their rear ends and cut it off with the shears. These were usually the ones with no top front teeth.

I did this every day, in blistering heat with nothing but Marmite sandwiches and a jar of tea for lunch. One stifling afternoon a huge cloud of flies hung over my head, the dogs lay under a tree panting and the sheep didn't even have the energy to try to escape. I remember tipping up yet another fly-blown old ewe and staring at her for the longest time. And that was when inspiration struck. I said to myself, "There are sixty million sheep in Australia. Maybe you should go back to school."

I do have some pleasant associations with sheep. Many years later back in Canada, I drove north out of the city one lovely March morning to visit with one of the neighbours just up the road from our old family farm. He and his daughter, a very attractive young woman with long brown hair tied up in a ribbon, were in the middle of lambing. I soon found myself out in the barn with the two of them, on my knees in the straw assisting with the delivery of twins. The young woman dried off one of the newborn lambs with a towel, held it up to her face and breathed it in.

"They have a wonderful smell," she exclaimed. "They smell new." Then she handed the lamb to me. I breathed it in. It smelled like poop to me.

But six months later I married that brown-haired shepherdess in the local church, and we've been keeping sheep ever since.

Granny Kate, 1912–2004

She went by a number of names, including Katie, Granny Dynamite and the Wildcat of the Marsh. She was born just before the *Titanic* sank and lived to see a spacecraft land on Mars. She was the centre of an elaborate network of family, friends and neighbours spread across the rural community where I live in southern Ontario. Katie Jordan—my wife's grandmother—was born in the log cabin her grandfather built in Proton Township. She knew backbreaking labour and grinding poverty for much of her early years. As a child she carried buckets of water from the creek on a yoke and milked nine cows by hand. She grew up a little stubborn, a little wilful, with a little bit of a temper—and she had her pride.

One evening while bringing the cows home she heard one moving through the underbrush out of sight. No matter how she cursed it and threw stones, it would not come out. After a bit she turned and counted her cows again and found she had all nine, and realized she was throwing stones at a black bear. Her father always said it was lucky for that bear that Katie didn't get it into her head that she was going to milk it.

She married a big, strapping man named Bill Jordan in 1932. They made an odd couple, such a tiny woman beside this big, burly man. Bill learned to duck early in the marriage, for Katie had a habit of throwing things when provoked: crockery, brooms and, once, a pitcher of sour milk. In 1938 they built a frame house using lumber cadged from the sawmill where Bill worked part-time. The cash outlay for that house was seven dollars—for nails, hinges, panes of glass and a doorknob.

They scratched a living at one thing and another until Bill landed a full-time job as a lineman with the Noisy River Telephone Company in 1943 and they were able to buy a farm on the Mad River outside Creemore. Bill founded Jordan's Gun Club in a little shed back by the river. It quickly became a local institution with its own Coke machine, a ceremonial cannon and parts for every weapon made since the invention of gunpowder.

Katie and Bill had a generous, open-handed way with visitors and continually took people in. There was always room at their table and a spare bed. "Put some more water in the soup, Mother. We have company!" was the family motto.

Bill's death in 1978 came as a shock to more than just his wife. I still meet grown men who get misty-eyed when they remember that man and his gun club. But Granny Kate carried on bravely. She sold the farm and moved into the village, where her life gradually found a new routine in gardening, neighbouring, coffee at the local diner and car trips to Alberta to stay in touch with her assorted grandchildren.

In later years we lost count of the spells that put her in hospital but, time after time, she defied all medical predictions and returned to her house and got back on her knees in the flower garden. Her little body finally just wore out, and she died peacefully in March.

Granny Kate was born before telephones, cars, electricity and central heating. She knew people who crossed the ocean in sailing ships and took the trees off the land. She was my last living witness to the pioneer days of Ontario.

When I see her in my mind's eye, she is standing in a kitchen (usually her own), putting food on the table (usually too much) and surrounded by children and dogs (usually too many). She was one of those people who became more remarkable as each year went by, because she managed to live at the centre of everything she loved.

In Search of the Great White Egg

My wife does not eat brown eggs. I found this out rather late in the game, after building a new hen house and installing a flock of rare Dominique chickens. Heath insists that brown eggs have more protein spots in them than white eggs. It's hard to dislodge her opinion once it has set, so I saved my breath and waited until we were at a big chicken conference and sought out the oracle himself, the poultry specialist from the University of Guelph.

"Perhaps you can clear up an old question in our household," I suggested. "Do brown eggs have more protein spots than white eggs?"

"No," he replied. "The only difference between white and brown eggs is the colour."

If I thought this was going to do the trick, I was mistaken. On the way home all Heath would say was, "He may be a clever man, but he doesn't know everything about eggs."

I have learned in seventeen years of marriage that two people can disagree on fundamental matters and still live happily together. After all, I have my own prejudices in the poultry department. For example, I don't like White Leghorns. They may be the darlings of the modern egg factory, but they're as jumpy as a bank clerk with his hand in the till, and there isn't enough meat on one bird for a chicken salad sandwich.

So I went off in search of the perfect white egg layer. I canvassed all the members of the Blue Mountain Poultry Club and discovered the Chantecler, the only Canadian breed of chicken. The Chantecler was invented in 1920 by a Trappist monk in the monastery at Oka, Quebec. For a time the breed was one of the most popular in Canada, because of its small combs that resisted freezing. I drove across the province for four hours and bought a breeding trio from a chicken enthusiast. Back at home they turned out to be lovely gentle things that stood around my feet clucking quietly. My hopes rose as I took the first eggs into the house.

"They're not white eggs," said my wife flatly.

"They're off-white. That's basically white, isn't it?"

It turns out that off-white is basically brown and does not pass the egg inspector in the kitchen. So I went on the internet and found the Araucana, a South American bird that lays a lovely whitish egg that is supposed to be low in cholesterol. Another year of incubation, brooding, feeding and watering gave me three hens and twenty-five roosters. Then I discovered that some of the Araucanas lay blue eggs, which again puts them squarely in the brown category, which by now is a basket by the door to be distributed to the poor.

Last year I went off to the Fur and Feather Show, which takes place every spring in the open air on the fairgrounds racetrack in the town of Mount Forest, Ontario. At the crack of dawn on Sunday morning, people eager to buy, sell and trade anything that walks, flies or slithers descend on this sleepy little town in hundreds of ancient pickup trucks, horse trailers, station wagons and camper vans. The sellers line both sides of the track with their displays and the buyers walk around the track. By the time the sun comes up there can be several thousand people on the grounds. And it's all over by noon. In the infield I struck up a conversation with a young man from down near Tillsonburg and told him about my quest.

"Black Minorcas," he said and pressed a carton of hatching eggs into my hand. This did not sound promising, I thought, as I handed some crumpled notes to him in return. It felt like a drug deal. But I took them home to the incubator and started reading about Minorcas. They come from Spain and have a lovely swoop to their tails. At one time they were the most popular white egg layer in North America but were displaced by the incredible output of the scrawny Leghorn.

All twelve eggs hatched. One hen and eleven roosters. The following spring the first egg appeared in the nest box in the henhouse. It was pure-as-the-driven-snow white. I took it into the kitchen and held my breath as my wife wiped it off, examined it very carefully—and put it in the fridge.

That was the last egg the hen produced that summer. I called the Minorca man and he laughed. "Minorcas are a show bird but they're not much of an egg layer anymore. Just in the spring and about one each."

As they say, you can't make an omelette, or a marriage, without breaking some eggs.

The Infernal Combustion Engine

I attended a conference last year at which the keynote speaker, a Silicon Valley guru, explained that the reason we're so frustrated with the home computer is that we're in the "disappointment phase of the technology." He insisted that new technologies don't actually take hold until they become "embedded," that is, until they accomplish simple tasks so reliably and so well that you aren't even aware of the technology at work. He suggested we think of the toaster. I remember thinking instead about the internal combustion engine and wondering if this man had ever owned a lawn tractor, a chainsaw or any of the labour-saving devices that owners of rural properties have relied on for a century or more.

My 1992 Bolens lawn tractor stopped turning to the right last month. This sort of thing always presents a challenge, because there is no one left in the country who stocks parts or really wants to work on my machine. Several hours after I took delivery, the company went out of business. After twelve years I know a lot of the machine's habits. It won't start without the gas and choke on full. It trips itself out of hydrostatic gear in tall grass. It inhales stuff through the electronic gizmo in the carburetor and wheezes along at half-power until I take it apart and blow the little gizmo out with an air hose.

But when something mechanical goes wrong, I'm in big trouble. First of all I have to stare at it for a very long time until my untutored eye locates the source of the problem. Every replacement part has to be fabricated in the local machine shop at great expense. Each breakdown brings me to the tipping point: Do I fix it or buy a new one? New ones are three times the price they were back in '92, so I now belong to a secret society of Bolens owners who talk to one another on the web and meet in Tim Hortons parking lots to exchange cash for parts in paper bags.

My latest clue was the "thunk" of a small missile that hit the doghouse while I was cutting the lawn. I got off the tractor and found a heavy two-inch brass shoulder bolt implanted in the wall. It looked like the kind of bolt you would use to hold two pretty important things together. I assumed the lotus position and studied the underside of the machine for a long time, but I could not see any obvious signs of pathology. The next day my son announced that the steering wouldn't work.

I languished in the disappointment phase of modern technology until the grass got to be eight inches high. Then I cancelled my appointments for the day and went to the barn with a copy of the Bolens repair manual I had purchased online from a shady mail-order house in New Jersey. I stripped the machine down, hoisted the front end off the ground and carefully examined the steering adjustment. It looked exactly as it was supposed to, just like in the manual. I twiddled the steering wheel back and forth to try to figure out what was wrong. Finally I noticed that although the tires didn't move, the whole front axle did. I looked closer and realized the axle wasn't actually attached to the tractor at all. There were four large holes in the frame where two-inch shoulder bolts had been at one time. The one that hit the doghouse must have been the last one to come undone.

My Bolens is back in service. It just has to cut the orchard once more before we put it away for the winter. I should be breathing more easily, but I noticed a small hole in the muffler today from which the odd blue flame appears. Of course, they don't make mufflers like that anymore.

Break a Leg

As the holiday season approaches, I am keenly aware that a number of Christmas pageants are now in production for various stages in the schools and community halls that dot our rural neighbourhood. Christmas just isn't complete for me without sitting on a squeaky wooden chair watching an amateur theatrical troupe bring an adaptation of *A Christmas Carol* to life. And they don't have to involve my own kids, because this kind of theatre is in my blood.

I grew up spending six months of the year in Rosemont, a tiny hamlet in the sandhills about an hour's drive northwest of Toronto. Rosemont is situated at the corner of four townships and straddles the boundary of two counties, which meant that it was routinely ignored by all of them. It took twenty-five years for the six municipal councils just to install a streetlight in the village, opposite the Orange Lodge Hall, and the residents soon found it saved a lot of trouble if they replaced the bulb themselves. But then, Rosemont had a long tradition of doing things on its own. It also had a long experience of entertaining itself.

When we arrived from the city in the mid-1950s, my mother, who was a teacher and wrote children's plays, decided that the community needed some live theatre. She had a bulldozer scrape the yard in front of our farmhouse into the shape of an outdoor stage and planted a screen of cedar hedging to mark the wing space and backdrop. Then she put out the word that she would be offering drama classes on Saturday mornings through the summer. Every week about two dozen farm kids left their chores and walked down the gravel road to our farm to be schooled in voice and movement, mime, dance and my favourite, stage fighting. She would write scripts for us, and on the last weekend in August another notice circulated in the community and the entire neighbourhood would interrupt the grain harvest to come down to the farm. They brought folding chairs, picnic lunches and babes in arms, and settled in to watch, until well after dark, a festival of one-act plays their children performed by the light of the headlights of cars parked in front of the stage.

As often happens with outdoor theatres, the elements persuaded us to seek shelter after a few seasons, and the festival moved up to the Orange Hall. Before long it was just understood that on all high holidays, such as the strawberry supper or the fowl supper, my mother's troupe of actors would provide the evening entertainment.

As I moved up through the ranks in the acting company, playing first a mushroom and then a wave and finally capturing a speaking part as third pirate, I gradually became aware that my mother's amateur theatre company was no exotic import from the big city. It actually fit seamlessly into a tradition that was long established in the Rosemont community.

Russell Thompson, the old carpenter from Mono Centre who built our farmhouse, remembered performing on the local stage back in the 1920s. He even recalled some of his lines, which included hoisting an axe on his shoulder and announcing to the audience that he was "goin' out to split some peas for the split-pea soup!" Even forty years later, tears rolled down his face as he remembered how the people whooped at his famous punchline.

It is a matter of pride that I launched my career as a professional playwright from Rosemont's Orange Hall stage in August 1984. My first play, *Letter from Wingfield Farm*, had its world premiere in front of about a hundred neighbours sitting on squeaky folding chairs, with the windows wide open to dissipate the stifling heat and the actor timing his lines so as not to be drowned out by the odd passing truck on the highway.

The local paper reported dutifully that "a good time was had by all," which is the closest you will ever get to a rave review in Rosemont.

And my mother ran the lights.

My Ecological Footprint

During the week my friend Peter lectures on environmental ethics at York University and then comes up to our farm on weekends to drink my Scotch and lecture me. We have enjoyed a long-running debate about green issues, and the current topic is the impact of our respective lifestyles on the natural world.

So far the city mouse is winning, hands down.

When my wife and I lived in the city, we owned a car but it sat in the parking lot for weeks at a time. We walked to work most days and spent our leisure time pursuing uplifting intellectual activities. But the city was noisy and crowded, and we were aching to live in closer harmony with nature. We dreamed of a little plot in the forest where we would take only what we needed from the land and tread lightly in the sun-dappled meadows beside softly lowing cattle and gentle sheep.

In 1988 we moved to the country, but the irony is that we now own two cars—and a pickup truck, a tractor, a lawn tractor, a lawnmower, a snow blower, a chainsaw, a whipper-snipper, a hedge trimmer, a diesel generator and a barbecue. Because we're five miles from town, we now spend most of our leisure time chauffeuring our kids around and rack up twenty-five thousand kilometres on each vehicle every year. Our consumption of hydro has jumped from three thousand kilowatt hours per year to more than thirty thousand. The cost of staying warm is now enormous because the heat from our energy-efficient oil furnace goes straight out through the roof of our century-old farmhouse.

Every day two big yellow school buses make two trips to our house. Every week two big trucks pick up my garbage. The mail and parcels come by car or truck, as does the oil, the firewood, the meter reader, the veterinarian, the dead stock wagon and every single visitor to the farm since 1988.

My friend is right. Ecologically the decision to move to the country has been a catastrophe. We were living like Trappist monks in that apartment compared with what we're doing now. We now use more fossil fuel than it would take to run a Chinese village. When I meet a couple from a high-rise in downtown Toronto, I should kneel and kiss the hem of their Italian suits and praise them for their deep commitment to environmental causes.

I do recycle. Every week I set out the kids' pop cans and my empty Scotch bottles, so I'm trying to do my bit. I have a compost pile too, but my friend says this is clearly not enough. He's done some calculations and reckons Canada could meet its obligations under the Kyoto Protocol in about two weeks if we ordered every hobby farmer like me back to the city and told them to stay put.

We were having this discussion last fall while digging postholes for a new fence around a wetland area. My friend was uncomfortable about the idea of pasturing this particular spot, because he was worried that the sheep would destroy much valuable biomass and the land would be degraded. "Why can't we ever live with a landscape as we find it?" he wailed. As he made his point, he paused to examine the dirt he had just turned over. He had dug into a ground nest of yellow jackets, and now they were boiling up out of the earth in large numbers. Ever the scientist, he bent over to look closer. "Hey, this is really neat!" he said.

"Run for your life!" I yelled and sprinted off toward the house. My Buddhist buddy passed me on the veranda going into the house, and we spent the next few minutes whacking each other with newspapers. Some time later we went back out with a can of gas and a pack of matches and conducted a scorched earth campaign against the ground bees.

There was no more discussion about our ecological footprint that weekend until I took him to the bus.

Riding My Pony Home

I t seems whenever I join the crowd of Old Guys at Rhonda's diner in the village, conversation inevitably drifts around to the good old days when everyone walked five miles to school, uphill both ways. As the youngest member of the group, I usually can't match any of these tales.

My neighbour, Mike Currie, was just telling me how he and his brother, Pete, and their two sisters, Mary and Ruth, all got to school in the 1940s on a workhorse named Polly. Polly would appear in the yard every morning and lower her head to the ground. One by one, each kid would grab hold of her ears, get hoisted up and slide down her neck into position. When Polly had all four kids lined up on her back, she would set off for the school about a mile away. Generally she came straight home after dropping them off. But if it was stormy, she'd go into the first barn and wait patiently there until the weather cleared or Mr. Currie came to collect her.

"Guess you never rode a horse to school, did you?" Mike chuckled.

In fact, I did ride a horse home from school, once, when I was fourteen. And I remember the adventure well, because the school was in Lakefield, Ontario, and home was 125 miles west, in Rosemont. The trip took five days and four nights, and it was uphill most of the way, from the bug-infested cedar swamps of the Kawartha Lakes to the bug-infested sand drumlins of Dufferin County. The horse was the tough little bay gelding named Tony that my mother had bought for me on the strict condition that I took care of it, including all expenses. Trucking Tony to school had cost me all of my tuck shop allowance for the first term, and I flinched at the idea of going into debt to get him home. So I saddled him up after the school closing ceremonies, tied a poncho and a sleeping bag behind me and trotted west.

Up to that point Tony had never walked anywhere in his life. He always ran. About fifteen miles west of Lakefield he finally slowed to a walk, and we spent the night under a spruce tree beside Chemong Lake. It had been a damp spring, and the mosquitoes were ferocious. The next morning we plodded on south of Lindsay, and the swamps gave way to the stony pastures and hardwood bush of Victoria County.

The year was 1965, and my route ran straight across a rural Ontario that was still largely made up of family farms. The second night I stopped at a dairy farm owned by Lloyd Kennedy near Little Britain. Mrs. Kennedy watched me laying out my bedroll in the orchard and shooed me into the house where she put me in the spare bedroom and insisted I telephone my mother to tell her where I was. The next day we reached Norm Bagshaw's farm in the hills north of Uxbridge, where I helped with the evening milking and went hunting groundhogs with his teenage son.* The day after I set off again in a heavy rain, slapping the mosquitoes on Tony's shoulders with a towel at every second step. The sun came out in the afternoon as we reached the vegetable farms of Holland Marsh. I forget the name of the pig farmer in Bradford who put me up on the fourth night, but I do remember going down to the sales barn with him to sell pigs and sitting up late to watch Johnny Carson.

The fifth day we crossed the sod farms south of Alliston, climbed up into the sandy hills of Dufferin County and made it home in time for supper.

That trek gave my horse a new outlook on life. He started saving his energy because he was never quite sure if I was going to make him walk all the way back to Lakefield someday. It changed me too. I got a view of the countryside and its easy hospitality that has stayed with me for forty years.

*The week after this column appeared, my editor was having some wiring redone in the house. The electrician turned to him at one point and said, "You know that story you ran about the guy who rode horseback across Ontario? Well, the kid he went shooting groundhogs with was me." It was Norm Bagshaw's son.

A Public Life

There are some drawbacks to living in a place where everybody knows your name. Whenever a truck turns down the Ninth Concession to deliver a piece of furniture or you nip out in your bathrobe to drive the kids to the bus, you know that windows are probably steaming up along the sideroad. Your life is a matter of public record.

I went to the local hospital recently for a colonoscopy, something I had hoped might remain a private matter between the surgeon and me. It turned out that all the nurses working around him could have formed a quorum for the Parents Council at my kids' school. It reminded me of one of those recurring bad dreams I have in which I'm standing in front of an audience without any clothes on. The only difference was that this was really happening.

I suppose that in some ways life in the country has changed very little over the years. In the days when small family farms lined the concession roads, everyone lived and worked in full view of their neighbours. Each family followed the same schedule of morning and evening chores, and all entered the same race against time and weather to plant and harvest the crops. It was a matter of public record when the lights came on in your barn in the morning, how well you maintained fences and how successfully you stored up hay and grain to carry your animals through six months of hard winter. A man was judged by the straightness of his furrow and a woman by her skill in the garden and kitchen.

Many of the community's sons and daughters took the first bus south to escape the harsh glare of publicity on the sideroads and shape their own destinies. They were rewarded with better-paying jobs in the city and relative anonymity. But they also gave up a circle of people that, whatever their faults, knew them better than anyone else.

Today some of those wanderers and their descendants are finding their way back to our old rural communities. If their experience is anything like mine, they are probably wondering how much privacy you are expected to give up in exchange for a sense of neighbourhood and belonging.

It's a difficult question and one that bothers even the older residents. They will tell you that the eyes of the neighbours served for more than a century as a pretty effective form of regulation of human behaviour in this township; in fact, they were probably a lot more effective than the parade of government-sponsored busybodies and do-gooders who now invade every nook and cranny of our lives.

I have an old dairy farmer friend who was grumping to me about all the boards, agencies and commissions he reports to and the army of officials who supervise his daily activities. "There's the milk marketing board, the conservation authority, the Niagara Escarpment Commission, the township bylaw enforcement officer, building inspectors, traffic cops, truck cops." He ran down the list shaking his head. "And they still say I need a wife to keep me in line!"

It's true: the neighbourhood telegraph does occasionally suffer a serious intelligence failure, like the CIA with the invasion of Iraq. But more often than not, it gets it spectacularly right. Lost dogs and cows are restored promptly to their owners. Storm warnings are issued, houses are checked, meals are delivered to shut-ins and wandering children are herded home safely. And pity the poor man who thinks he can toss a mattress into the ditch out here on the sideroad without being noticed.

For those who are worried about the destructive effects of rumour and hearsay, the solution, of course, is to lead an entirely blameless life. Either that or develop a thicker skin.

Working in Stone

I live in a land of glacial till, where the stones have been pounded so often by ice sheets that only the hardest ones have survived. They are generally round and impossible to split. But someone around here must have had the knack of working with them, because fieldstone farmhouses and barn foundations dot the township. Unfortunately the knack was not passed on to me.

One summer while I was still at university, I helped an Austrian stonemason named John Held build a large fireplace for the new Globe Restaurant in Rosemont. John was old enough to remember standing on a pier in Vienna a few years before the First World War watching Kaiser Wilhelm and Czar Nicholas cruise by on a yacht. I acted as his personal forklift on stone-hunting expeditions through the pastures of Mono Township, rolling boulders over for him to examine and wrestling them up a plank onto the back of the truck. For John the material we were sorting fell into two categories: "good shtone" and "no-good shtone." He would point to a spot on a likely boulder and tell me to hit it right there with the sledge. After a couple of whacks it usually fell into two pieces. After a few days of this I decided I'd got the hang of it and tried selecting a boulder of my very own. I pounded on it for ten minutes until John came over, took one look at it and said, "Bah! No-good shtone."

John didn't like the smooth, shiny ones in solid dark colours. But there were lots of other stones that looked very fireplace friendly to me, lovely pink and blue granites and white quartzes that he would dismiss without explanation. I tried to squeeze some of the secrets of the trade out of him, but he was not much of a talker on the job. After work he always sat me down at his kitchen table, poured ice-cold schnapps into shot glasses and told stories about the old country. The art of splitting stone remained a mystery.

On my own farm a fallen-in foundation in the front yard marks the spot where the old farmhouse once stood. A couple of summers ago I decided to resurrect the stones near the surface and build an ornamental garden wall. My friend Steven Thomas, who was trying to get a play out of me at the time and is used to coaxing play-wrights through writer's block, offered to help. Steve turned out to be another mason *manqué*. The two of us donned safety glasses, rented a cement mixer and proceeded to pound the pile of stones to gravel with our sledgehammers.

Over the course of the week a rustic wall emerged out of the rubble (and so did the plot for the play). On the Sunday my father-in-law dropped by on his way to see a man about a bull and joined us for a beer on the veranda. I pointed to our handiwork on the front lawn and asked him what he thought.

He glanced at it briefly. "I've got a broken down bitch of a wall like that myself at home," he sighed. "I've got to do something about it one of these days."

"But, Don," I protested. "We just built it!"

"Oop," he said, wincing. "I guess that wasn't what you wanted to hear."

The wall still isn't finished. It needs a top and the joints are pretty rough, but the climbing roses and the daylilies help. Father has decided he likes it after all and has asked me to take a look at the corner of his barn foundation. Apparently it could use the attention of a free mason.

The Perfect Gift

I t was a charming little bracelet of red carnelians set in antique gold and patterned on an ancient Etruscan design. My wife bought it in a jewellery store in the hill town of Volterra in rural Tuscany on a trip we made there for our fifteenth anniversary. And she was very upset one day last summer when the clasp broke and it fell off her wrist somewhere in town. We retraced her steps and looked everywhere, but the bracelet was lost.

She shrugged and said, as she always does, it's just a thing and things can be replaced. Then it struck me that Christmas was coming and here was a golden opportunity to come up with the perfect gift. After eighteen years of marriage I know that nothing is more important to domestic harmony than The Christmas Present. I remembered the name of the jewellery store, and it took me only a few moments to find it on the internet. I scrolled through the store's list of products and found that the very same bracelet was still being made. As luck would have it, some friends of ours were jetting off to Sorrento that very week, and they offered to bring the bracelet home for me if I could get it delivered to their hotel. The stars were aligning in my favour.

The people at the store wouldn't answer emails, however, and when I called them directly, nobody behind the counter spoke

English. Undaunted, I snuck into town and went to see my friend Marina who was born in Italy and speaks the language fluently. I found her sitting in her kitchen with a couple of friends. As I explained the situation, the ladies wilted in admiration.

"How romantico!" cried Marina. "Of course, I will do this. She will love it!"

Marina hopped on the telephone to Volterra, and I listened to a few minutes of spirited conversation in Italian. Yes, the store could deliver the bracelet and yes, it would be there in lots of time before my friends had to fly back. I handed Marina my credit card to clinch the deal. There was a pause before she turned to me and said, "So sorry, they don't take credit cards."

"What about a wire transfer?" I suggested. Marina then translated and wrote down three bank transfer numbers, each one longer than the serial number on my car. I dashed off to the bank.

We're asked to believe that we live in a global village with instant access to one another, but when you actually try to arrange a currency transaction between a small-town Italian jewellery store and a rural Ontario bank, you are hurled back in time to the days of crank telephones and steamer trunks. After several failed attempts to match the numbers, the teller shrugged.

"It will probably go through," she said doubtfully. "We can put a trace on it in ten days to find out if it got there."

I hesitated, which is always fatal to romance. Launching money into cyberspace on the wobbly assumption that it would navigate the bank labyrinth, leap over the language barrier and synchronize with the Italian postal system, all in the space of five days, seemed like a stretch. Alas, the course of true love never runs smooth. I went home to rethink the operation.

My wife found me preoccupied as we sat on the veranda, sipping a late-morning latte from her little Italian espresso machine. The oak leaves in the garden had turned, and the first frost had wilted the geraniums in the planter hanging from the veranda railing beside my chair. I absently picked at the dead blossoms and noticed the sun glint off something shiny beside my hand. I looked closer. There in the soil was the little carnelian bracelet. She had been watering a hanging pot, and the bracelet must have slipped off and dropped into the planter.

I am suffering from mixed emotions, like the man watching his mother-in-law drive off a cliff in his new Cadillac. It's wonderful to have the bracelet back, but it was such an inspired idea for a Christmas present. I have only a few weeks to think of something else.

Country Kids and City Kids

M y childhood was divided between a house in the city and a hardscrabble pasture farm my mother used as a writer's retreat for the warmer six months of the year. It was an odd existence. Every spring my mother would pack her five children and assorted dogs, cats and other baggage into an old St. John's Ambulance van and move us an hour out of the city to Rosemont, where she wrote novels and plays and kept a herd of Jersey cows. She enrolled us in the local two-room school and put us to work doing barn chores and, when we got older, fieldwork for the neighbouring farmers.

We all loved the annual remove to the farm and, forty years later, four of my brothers and sisters still make their lives in the country. (I'm the only one who keeps sheep and cattle.) The sister who chose to remain in the city regularly dispatches her children to at least one of her siblings' rural properties every summer to give them a taste of the life she knew as a child.

It's a well-worn notion that country kids tend to be more self-reliant and practical, if perhaps somewhat easier to fool, than their street-smart city cousins, who in turn don't know where eggs come from and can't find the reset switch on the furnace. I do not adhere to this hoary idea, perhaps because my own four children, all raised in the same place, with virtually identical influences, show dramatically different scores on their naïveté and practicality charts.

I have found that babies arrive with fully formed personalities that defy classification. Scientists think we all follow genetic railroad tracks to become the sort of person we turn out to be, whether we're raised on a farm or a houseboat on the Yangtze River. Someday they will get a clearer picture of those tracks.

Our vet was raised in a suburb and recalls no connection to farm life. But he knew from an early age that he wanted to look after large animals in the country. Another friend who was raised on a hog farm bolted at the first opportunity and headed for zero lot-line comfort in the city, where his partner changes the light bulbs for him.

The farmer next door watched my mother trying to cope on her own with three boys and advised her, "Just give them a collie dog and a .22 rifle and they'll raise themselves." That's just what she did. She also gave me a horse and told me not to hang around the house so much. I roamed the family farm with rod and gun until I knew every fold in the land, every bend in the creek, every stump and stone pile on our place and the four surrounding farms. But I was like that in the city too. I bicycled for miles with my friends, rambled through ravines and rode the subway by myself in a way that would horrify an urban parent today. I'm very lucky that my mother was not easily horrified. By the time I was nineteen my wanderings had already taken me across Canada, down through the South Pacific, around the Australian outback and on a cycling tour of Europe.

I have two grown nephews who were raised in the tiny hamlet of Rosemont. The family joke is that Andrew needed a forty-piece band to keep him entertained while Christopher could amuse himself with a rubber band. My wife was a farm girl who learned as a preschooler how to amuse herself in an open field. She and her sister were fairy princesses weaving flower garlands deep in the magic forest of burdock and thistle trees.

So is there a difference between farm-raised and city-grown kids? I daresay if they had not been raised on the farm, my wife would probably not sleep with three dogs in the bed and her sister would not have a pet turkey that sits with her on the couch and watches television. But then again, I'm not so sure. After all, they are who they are.

Horses and Happy Endings

I have written about the various animals that have been dropped off at our little farm over the past twenty years. There have been any number of stray dogs and cats, kindergarten chicks and rabbits, and out-of-fashion breeds of cattle, sheep and goats. Each one of them had a story and, for the most part, they have had happy endings.

Take old Zoey, for example, the Appaloosa mare that was dumped off about nine years ago, supposedly because she was "a dear old thing who needed a place to retire." The longer we kept her, the more stories we heard about her past. She had been kicked out of just about every stable in Simcoe County for fence jumping, stall chewing and generally unsociable behaviour. It's not that she's mean. She just lacks empathy. We tried several companion horses with her, but she was so unpleasant to all of them that we decided she could just live by herself. Now that she is thirty-two, she shows no signs of mellowing, or expiring, for that matter. In her crabby way she seems quite happy.

Possibly because they live so long the horses seem to have the most interesting stories. Early in 1995 Ken Driver, an old horseman and storyteller who worked behind the counter at the local building supply, asked me if I would be interested in a horse. His wife, Karen, kept a thirteen-year-old dapple grey gelding named Joe at her father's farm, but her dad was then approaching eighty and was getting too frail to look after horses. Karen had raised Joe from a colt and wanted him to go to a good home.

Joe was an enormous horse but very gentle. He turned out to be an explorer, and I enjoyed hacking over the hills around the farm with him for the next two years. It was like riding around on a big white sofa. Unfortunately he developed an abscess in his front right hoof and became very touchy about having his feet handled. Even after the foot had healed he developed a nasty habit of striking out with that foot if you tried to pick it up.

I'm a writer, not a horseman, and I made the difficult decision to send Joe out west to my brother-in-law, Dewy Matthews, who runs a guiding and outfitting ranch in Turner Valley, Alberta. I think Ken and Karen were a little upset with me that Joe was going to do trail rides, but I knew Joe needed the attention of a professional before he hurt somebody. Dewy cured the foot sensitivity problem and Joe took to mountain horseback

adventure with enthusiasm. He quickly shed two hundred pounds and, by the time I saw him next, he was in the best shape of his life. Whenever I took the family out for a visit to Turner Valley, I got to take Joe for breathtaking rides through the mountain passes.

When Joe hit twenty, Dewy retired him out of the hills, and the horse now does light duty around the ranch, carrying the minister for horseback weddings and following the hayrides to watch for stragglers. Last December Dewy trailered him into northwest Calgary at the request of a young man who dressed up as a knight in shining armour and rode into a schoolyard to ask for the hand of a pretty young schoolteacher. All the students and teachers cheered when she accepted his proposal. She cried, of course, and Joe played the part of the faithful charger beautifully.

Dewy sent me the pictures, and I forwarded them to Karen. Ken passed away four years ago, but I know he would have been just thrilled to see another horse story with a happy ending. Not that it's necessarily the end of Joe's story. After all, Zoey is a full ten years older and hasn't lost her appetite for life. She's eaten all the top rails off the barnyard fence and is starting on the east wall of the barn.

But that's another story.

A Thirtieth-Anniversary Event Planner

Having married into a very large extended farm family in 1987, I have some experience with how anniversary parties are arranged in rural Canada. First thing you do is put a notice in the Coming Events section of *The Gleaner*, saying that you're having a come-and-go tea at the house on a date a month from now and everybody is welcome.

When you get home you sit at the kitchen table for a minute and reflect on how shabby the place looks. A wave of panic will sweep over you, and you will get on the phone to all your married daughters and female relations, including your mother, to start planning the menu.

Right about then Father makes a growling noise from his chair beside the wood stove, sounding something like a truck going uphill in low gear. It is important to give him one simple task to complete before the big day, something that is not too demanding but will make him feel a part of the preparations, such as fixing that broken step coming into the back kitchen.

In week two you will be seized with an irrational urge to redo the front room, which hasn't had a coat of paint since you were married. Uncle Ed offers to come down Friday and do the job, but a crew will be needed to move all the furniture out for him.

Your sons-in-law volunteer to come down on Thursday night to manhandle everything out to the drive shed in the dark. One of them twists an ankle on that broken step, prompting Father to say irritably that he will "get to it."

So now it's week three. The front room is still unpainted, and Uncle Ed is in North Bay for the opening of the pickerel season. The materials for the kitchen step are sitting where they were dropped off by the hardware store, but the crew is now out "on the fields" with the good weather and not expected to return until it rains. Meanwhile you're thinking of engaging a professional mediator to intervene with your daughters, who are locked in mortal combat over the menu. The belt's off the lawnmower and the lawn's half done. The place is a shambles.

The very day before the great event you wake up to find a motorhome in the laneway. It's your cousins from the Maritimes who have driven all the way without stopping "to surprise you." By noon the yard is full of trucks, one of which belongs to Uncle Ed, who has finally brought the paint. The work party swells through the day and includes Father's closest friends, who arrive with a backhoe and go to work on that step. At midnight you flop down on the bed exhausted, wondering what on earth made you think this was a good idea.

You rise in the morning to find that the men have been up pretty much all night. The front room is painted and the furniture is back in. The wooden steps are gone entirely, replaced by a vast stone patio, which looks really nice. Your daughters arrive, freighting in food, new lamps for the living room, a set of drapes, flowers and planters. At ten o'clock the first guests arrive.

Now, if you've driven up from the city because of the notice you saw in the paper last month, you watch the day unfold and ask, "Wasn't this just a tea?" The tables are piled high with cold cuts, pickles, salads, breads, cheese trays, pies and cakes. Cars line both sides of the concession road right down to the highway. Every room of the house is jammed with people, and they spill out to the picnic tables in the yard. There's music and laughter. You feel like everyone you've ever known in your life is right there. It feels wonderful.

The Great Divides

It used to be that I had to drive into Toronto to feel like I wasn't making enough money. Now I can get that feeling just by driving into Collingwood, the little town ten minutes away that has recently exploded as a "four seasons" leisure and retirement community.

Since 1978 I have watched at least three panic sell-offs in our local property market, the first of which occurred about three days after I bought this farm. The present real estate rocket ride is proving to be more durable, but since my little farm is located in the Back Settlement, which is about a million dollars south of the monster neo-colonial ski chalets and gated condo developments that cluster along the shoreline of Nottawasaga Bay, our lives have not changed. I can see the culture of Starbucks, Wi-Fi and sodium lights encroaching now from both horizons north and south of us, but it hasn't yet reached my doorstep.

We still have a mailbox, a septic tank, two wells and a wood stove, all the scout badges of rural life. We even had a party telephone up until a few years ago. We shared it with Kenny Jardine, the bachelor farmer across the road, until he moved into town to escape the howling snowstorms that tumble off the escarpment and sweep down across the flats.

I remember working on a television project in the city as a scriptwriter about ten years ago, when the line producer called me up and asked for my fax number so she could send me a list of the director's script changes. I told her I didn't own a fax.

"Well, get one," she snapped. I explained that a fax machine does not work on a party line.

"What?" she said incredulously. "Do they pave the roads up there?"

She rang off, and I sat there wondering if I was finally going to have to abandon what had become my own early form of the internet chat room. Every morning I could pick up the phone and log on with Kenny and Helen Kenwell for all the news between Nottawa and Maxwell: births, deaths, barn fires, car crashes, farm mishaps, crop failures and rabid foxes. I would miss the colour and the commentary of those morning newscasts.

Fortunately the producer called me back a few minutes later to say that the director had taken a second look at the script and decided the changes weren't really necessary after all. I thanked her and rang off, making a mental note never, ever to buy a fax machine as long as I was working in television.

They have just installed a signal in town that is supposed to give me high-speed internet access, but there is a row of spruce trees along the Jardine Sideroad that blocks our view of the tower, and we still limp along with dial-up, something the children have learned to detest. Cell phones don't work in the nearby valley villages and if the wind is howling at night, the satellite TV signal disappears completely. The scan button on the car radio often goes round and round the dial without picking up a single station. The only reliable distraction on such nights is the crokinole board, just as it was when my wife and I were children.

So the divide between city and country may be narrower geographically, but in many ways it remains just as sharp as ever. The schools in town are bursting at the seams, though enrolment continues to drop at the country school on the hill. It has divided its classes into "splits" so often that it is now effectively a two-room school, something not seen in this part of the world since the 1960s.

My nine-year-old daughter is doing a project on the pioneers, from whom she considers herself to be directly descended. She has solemnly informed her reading public that her parents used to play with cornhusk dolls and did their lessons on a slate. Her delusion on this point is completely understandable.

The Slow Food Chain

This plot of ground should be hugely productive. Every year I fatten lambs, pigs and a steer for the freezer. The orchard produces apples, pears and plums. I keep a flock of laying hens and a large garden. But there always seems to be some hiccup between the barn and the kitchen table.

I milked a cow and two goats for several years until the kids eventually turned their noses up at their milk in favour of the store-bought variety. Our free-range chickens were so tough they had to be simmered for several hours before you could eat them. My wife doesn't eat lamb, and my daughter has become a vegetarian. A single spray of the orchard now costs seventeen dollars, which would buy enough apples at the local market to last us all winter.

My wife long ago returned to the supermarket to ensure a stable food supply in our house and, about a year ago, she began buying omega-3 milk and eggs. Some television host convinced her that we need extra linoleic acid in our diet to reduce the incidence of heart attack and stroke. I was a skeptic until I attended the Farmsmart Conference at the University of Guelph last winter, where an eminent professor said exactly the same thing and tipped me off that I could produce my very own omega-3 eggs just by feeding flaxseed to my hens.

On the way home I picked up a bag of flax at the feed store and added it at the rate of one big scoop to a fifty-pound bag of lay mash. Then I sat back and waited for the health benefits to roll in. Of course, the effects aren't immediate. It takes about ninety days for the stuff to work its way through to the eggs, which is a long time in the life of a chicken around here. Then, just as the eggs were reaching their maximum omega-3 potency, a family of skunks burrowed under the henhouse and started swiping the eggs. I plugged that hole and some raccoons quickly made another one, ate several hens and traumatized the flock so badly that they stopped laying altogether. So the eggs didn't actually make it to the table, but the local raccoon and skunk populations appear to be healthier than ever.

This is often the way it goes out here. I have lost count of those failed enterprises that began with some "Aha!" moment late at night in bed while I leafed through some obscure poultry magazine. "I wish you'd read *Penthouse* like other husbands," says my wife.

I now have three breeds of chickens. I bought Araucanas first because they lay those blue-shelled eggs that are supposed to be cholesterol free, if you believe the promotional literature that comes with them. Next I invested in Chanteclers, a breed developed here in Canada to thrive in very cold temperatures. A rooster's comb is the source of his fertility, and the very small combs of the Chantecler resist freezing. Finally I found Cornish game hens that are dual-purpose and will actually set and hatch the eggs of the other two breeds.

None of this is working the way I planned. Although the Chanteclers do lay an egg now and then, their rooster froze his comb last winter and has been shooting blanks ever since. The Araucana rooster drowned himself in the horse trough after Dougie, the visiting pot-bellied pig, performed certain unspeakable acts on him late one night. The Cornish rooster is intact and enthusiastic, but his mate is not laying any eggs at all after that raccoon incident. She has been sulking silently on a dish of cat kibble for over three months now.

My wife says you know there is a problem in the laying flock when you hear yourself saying that you're going out to the henhouse "to get the egg."

The professor insists that health benefits delivered directly in our food—or "nutraceuticals" as they are called—are the exciting new wave of the future in food production. For the moment, however, we will have to make do with a spoonful of cod liver oil at breakfast.

My Cuban Crop Tour

M y wife says I'm the only person who can spend a week at a Caribbean beach resort without ever taking off his shoes.

I prefer to walk, generally in the other direction from the canned salsa music and the rum-sodden louts at the pool bar. This time we are in Cuba, and I notice a gardener struggling with mattock and spade to remove the root of an old banana tree from a garden near the front lobby. He straightens up and grins, and we chat for a minute in the international language of crops and the weather. He tells me how much they need the rains after five years of drought. Nearby a young man sits on a bench beside his horse and cart, ready to ferry the tourists down to the craft market in town. He introduces himself as Gisnay and quickly determines that crafts are not at the top of my list.

"Would you like to see a farm?" he asks.

Do bananas grow on trees? The next morning we set off at a brisk trot in the stifling heat, and the scenery gives way to lush pastures. On the edge of town he turns the surprised horse right instead of the usual left, down a lane past tiny concrete-block houses. Everyone waves at us, much like they do back in my home-town in Canada.

"You seem to know everybody," I say.

"Yes," Gisnay laughs, "but these are all the people that I know."

Another turn and we are on a dirt track leading up to a cluster of buildings and shade trees on a rise looking over the town. We are in a barnyard that reminds me of Mono Township back in southern Ontario, circa 1955. A dog gets up, wagging his tail. Chickens are everywhere. An enormous pig sleeps in the shade of a thatched hut. Gisnay introduces me to Armelio, a man of about seventy who's wearing a machete on his belt, and motions me through a gate held together by scraps of wire and string. He is taking me on a crop tour.

Armelio knows no English, but my young guide translates. My host feeds his extended family of about twenty-five people from this fifteen-acre plot. He leads me through a small plantation of bananas and explains the different varieties he grows. We inspect a plot of black beans, and he yanks a plant out of the ground to show me the roots of a yam and pulls a cob off a stalk of sweet corn to let me taste the kernels. There's an orchard of mango, guava and orange trees, a garden with pumpkins, sweet potatoes and tomatoes. He shows me an ancient stone-lined well with just a few feet of muddy water at the bottom. But he seems pleased that the rains have finally recharged it. There's a flock of brown goats in the pasture and several turkeys. The cropland is a reddish brown soil that clumps up nicely in the hand and crumbles between my fingers. Up on the knoll above the house, however, it turns to hardpan clay, just like I have at home.

"Hard ground," I say sympathetically, and he points to a kiln where he fires bricks, using clay dug from this knoll. The family is building a new house for one of his many grandsons. A birthday party is in progress in one of the houses nearby, and a boy scampers over with a bottle of rum. The three of us drink a toast in the pigpen beside two hogs he is fattening for the table. The old man grins when I tell him he may be talking to the last man in Canada who does the same thing.

"We are farmers," he says and shakes my hand. I thank him for his time and hand him a bag of soaps, medicines, candy and other

Cuban rarities my wife has prepared for him, and climb back into the cart.

On the way home it occurs to me I may have stumbled on the perfect compromise for these snowbird vacations we take. Perhaps I could hoe beans and chop sugar cane for Armelio while my wife suns by the pool at the hotel.

I wonder if they have a diner in the village.

Farm-Sitters

T he wind out here on the Ninth Concession is unbelievable. People come to visit on a winter evening and laugh. They hang onto trees trying to make it to our front door and when they get their breath back they say, "There wasn't any wind in town!" That's because they have trees and buildings in town. If they didn't, they would learn to play a lot of crokinole, just like we do.

After listening to the wind howl in the eaves for three months, we always try to get away someplace. This isn't easy, because leaving a farm for a few days takes the same kind of planning and coordination as the evacuation from the Gallipoli beachhead. I fill the bale feeders and set up automatic watering systems for the live-stock in the barn. I put a foot-long stick of millet in Gnasher the love-bird's cage and drive the dogs up to the doggy bed and break-fast. But I still have to find some reliable person to watch over the place.

For many years I relied on Kenny Jardine, a retired bachelor farmer across the road who would supervise our absences. After Kenny moved into town, we stumbled on a young couple who live in a cramped basement apartment in the city and always jump at the chance to escape to the countryside. Kim and Peter are calm, observant people who get along very well with our kids. Last winter the couple offered to farm-sit for our very first adults-only Caribbean getaway.

My mother used a farm-sitter for her country property for many years when we were growing up. His name was Ron Tyrell and he lived across the street from us in the city. Ron knew absolutely nothing about milking cows or feeding chickens, but he was an expert at dealing with hysteria. He was a driving instructor by day, his wife was a fairly excitable fashion designer and they had three daughters who harboured ambitions for the stage. Ron would come out to the farm, install himself in a lawn chair with a gin and tonic and give the same response to every question: "I have complete confidence in your ability to solve this problem. Let me know how it turns out."

I always wondered why my mother would leave the farm in the care of a man who wore Bermuda shorts and sandals and never went near the barn. Much later I came to understand that she loved him because whenever she called from the other side of the Atlantic to ask him how things were going, he would always say breezily, "Oh, wonderful. Just fine."

Our beach resort had an odd system for delivering messages. Three arrived from Peter on the same day, in the wrong order, as the letters from the Russians to President Kennedy did during the Cuban missile crisis. The desk clerk handed me the first one, which apologized for the damage to the truck. The second one, which I found on the bedside table, assured me that the situation was under control and I shouldn't worry. My wife handed me the third one, which reported that the cow was gone and what should they do?

It turned out that a calf I was fattening had jumped out of the barnyard and escaped. Kim and Peter gave chase in the pickup, cornered it in Jim Ferguson's barnyard next door and somehow got it loaded. When they tried to unload it into the pen at home, the steer clambered right out over the racks, slid off the cab and took the side mirror off. But they captured it.

Peter was concerned I would be upset about the damage to the truck. In fact, I was speechless with admiration that two town kids had wrestled a five-hundred-pound animal onto a truck without a ramp. As far as I was concerned, they were the find of the decade.

Taking a cue from President Kennedy, I chose to reply to the first message Peter had sent. "I have complete confidence in your ability to solve the problem," I wrote. "Let me know how it turns out."

The Sixty-Thousand-Dollar Dog

My wife says that she remembers the moment she decided to marry me. I came to stay overnight at her family farmhouse, and at bedtime her little brown dog scampered up the stairs to the guest room to spend the night with me. I ended up sleeping with that dog pretty much every night for the next ten years. He's long gone now, but I still feel his weight in the bed beside me. He needed more covers than anyone.

Andy was a country dog, one of five puppies born in my wife's parents' bedroom, the offspring of an odd-looking Jack Russell and something else, possibly an alligator. The terriers roamed the farm like a motorcycle gang, fought ruthlessly under the dinner table and sang "Edelweiss" together on the couch whenever Father picked up the accordion.

Andy was devoted to us, in a psychotic sort of way. He was a high-strung dog who trembled with excitement, even when he was asleep. He lived a life of danger and needed a hundred acres to find it. He had a vocabulary of over a hundred words, most of it profanity learned from me. I pulled him out of countless scrapes and eventually stopped taking him into town because of his habit of walking up to a dog ten times his size and saying, "Your sister eats field mice." He had more scars and dents on him than a farm truck.

Andy's cheerfulness sprang from a complete absence of judgment. Like an officious government inspector with a clipboard and a Luger at the hip, he was forever imposing his narrow view of order on a chaotic world, which meant ridding it of every rodent, snake, visiting dog or meter reader that happened onto the property. Height was important to him. Children could pass freely, but anyone over five feet had to stop and present papers.

Fortunately, he never bit anyone, but he sure looked like he might. If anyone, including me, moved too fast around him, he would grab a pant leg and hold on until things slowed down. He thought our little Toyota was a Mercedes and if a person so much as touched it while he was inside, he would hit the window, snarling and slavering like Old Yeller in the final throes. People would jump back in fright and offer to take a cab. But as soon as I opened the door he would jump about and lick everyone's face, then sit on the nervous passenger's lap, with both front feet on the dash, and scan the road for illegal rabbit activity all the way home.

We called him the sixty-thousand-dollar dog because it was Andy who persuaded me to give up my job in the city and settle here on the farm. We tried smuggling him into our no-pets apartment building, but it was like trying to walk into a party unnoticed with Eddie Murphy on a leash. And so we packed up and left to raise our children in the Pretty River Valley, two hours north of the city and a half an hour away from Andy's brothers, which suited him fine.

People warned us about the dog becoming jealous when the first baby arrived. But Andy had a soft spot in his dark heart for the young of all species, even rabbits. He curled up in the playpen and snarled at anyone who leaned too close to coo. In time the babies wore all the fur off his ears and pulled out his grey whiskers one by one. His feet became rich with the smells of the farm. My wife said the pads of his feet smelled like popcorn and his ears like honey buckets. The rest of him often smelled like dead groundhog.

He's been gone ten years, but if you look closely at the ancient wool blanket my wife throws over us at night, you can still find a stray hair from that little brown dog. He sleeps with us still.

You Name It

I have always envied those owners of country properties who manage to settle on a name for their place and paint it in large letters across the barn a week after they take possession. After twenty-nine years, we have only recently started calling our place Larkspur Farm and only because a salesman pinned us down one day when he sold us a framed photo of the farm taken from the air.

"Larkspur Farm" seemed safe enough. The pink and blue flowers have been close to my heart ever since I grew them as a child in a little corner of my mother's garden. One year I showed them in a glass jar at the Beeton Fair and won a prize. I still grow masses of them in the beds on either side of the gangway of the big barn. And it's the name I gave to the capital of fictional Persephone Township in my Wingfield Farm plays. The name seemed to meet all the criteria: it wasn't pretentious or precious, it drew on a natural feature of the landscape and it held some personal significance (to me, at least).

But then I drove out in public with the name painted on the side of my truck and some know-it-all immediately informed me that wild larkspur is poisonous to cattle and is listed as a noxious weed in at least four provinces. "Why would you call your farm that?" he demanded.

I told him it was my wife's choice and that I had always wanted to call it the "Blind Line Cash and Cattle Company."

"But you don't have any cattle!" he snorted. I don't have any cash either.

I have helped others find names for their properties. My neighbour, Bob King, bought a farm and told me with great excitement that there must be over a hundred snapping turtles in the pond. "I think I'll call it 'Snapping Turtle Farm,'" he announced proudly.

"I'm thinking resale here, Bob," I cautioned. "Have you seen anything else on the pond?" He thought for a moment and remembered that he had seen a snowy egret . . . once, flying over the farm next door. The last I heard, he was still calling it "Snowy Egret Farm."

If you are thinking of formally registering your farm name, forget it. Whatever you choose has already been taken by some horse person. Way back in 1958 the police stopped my mother when she was driving the panel truck that she used for moving pigs, poultry and children. The officer warned her that the law required her to have her farm name and address displayed clearly on the door of the truck. She selected "Haystack Farm" and then discovered there was already a horse farm under that name. So she went to a Gaelic dictionary and came up with "Stuc án Fhier" which literally translates as "hill of grass." My Uncle Fred used to say she was "Stuck on Fear Farm!"

Uncle Fred had a country property too, but I don't remember it having a name. He built an elaborate fieldstone entrance with a shingled roof, radio-operated iron gates and a large wooden coat of arms sporting the motto "Pas de Jambon Vendredi" on the scroll below the shield. As a security measure, it failed dismally. The radio on the township road grader opened the gates every time it went by.

The whole discussion about names is silly really, because whatever we choose, the neighbours will still continue to call it by the name of the last farmer that died in the house. My farm has been the "Old Currie Place" ever since James Currie expired in the master bedroom in 1965. Before that it was the "Jardine Farm," a reference to the pioneer who gave up the ghost in the log cabin that used to stand in the orchard. Mr. Jardine apparently called it the "Jesuit Farm" in tribute to a missionary who was clubbed to death by the Iroquois here in 1649.

Someday, down at the diner in the village, someone may eventually refer to this property as the "Old Needles Place." Unfortunately I won't be around to hear it.

Farewell My Lovely

T he old red truck is no longer with us. After sixteen years of hauling hay, livestock, feed and garbage here on the farm, she entered into rest on May 17, 2007, and was committed to the Creemore scrapyard in a small service attended by a few friends.

Since it came off the line in 1983, the Ford has circled the globe eight times and received two body jobs, six mufflers, five brake jobs and a myriad of plugs, points and condensers. Retired out of the Hamilton Construction Company fleet in 1991, she got a fresh coat of red paint and took her place in front of the garden by the old barn, where she has been parked ever since.

The truck never needed a key to start it. You just had to twist the ignition switch and it would go. The neighbours came to appreciate this feature, and I often came home to discover that my truck was out in the community, busily doing good. It was an American truck, however, and every so often, without warning, it would suddenly decide to beef up security and demand the key, usually when you were in town and the key was hanging in the kitchen. This happened to my wife just recently, the same day Hamilton's called to advise that another of their trucks was being retired out of the fleet and was I ready yet? The combination proved fatal to the Ford.

My friend Bob Burns drove up to help me through her final day. He followed in his car at a discreet distance as we took our last drive together down River Road to Creemore. The wild apples were in full bloom, the birds sang in the fencerows and the groundhogs stood to attention by their burrows as we passed. Sixteen years is a big part of a person's life. My children have never known the farm without that red truck, although my daughter has refused to be seen publicly in it for years. "It's so welfare, Dad!" she moaned the last time I tried to drop her off at the high school. She made me let her out two blocks away and never rode in it again.

The guys in the diner in the village called her the Iron Eagle because of the way the side panels gently flapped on a trip down the highway. On our final voyage one mudguard broke loose from the panel and skittered off into the ditch. Bob stopped, gathered it up and tossed it in the back.

"It is time, Dan," he said to me, not unkindly. He looked like Gandalf and I felt like Frodo.

That he was right did not make it easier. This was the last truck Ford made with a carburetor. Everything nowadays is fuel injected, computerized and hostile to the do-it-yourselfer.

At the scrapyard a young face popped out of the booth beside the weigh scales.

It was Wayne Gordon, a graduate of my 4-H Beef Club. "My, my!" he said in wonder. Even a scrap dealer has a heart, and Wayne paused for a moment as he watched a little bit of his childhood pass by. He weighed the truck and handed me $196. Scrap is a good price these days because it goes straight to China where they have no environmental restrictions about burning painted metal.

"She'll probably come back to you someday in a steel-belted radial tire," joked Wayne as he sliced through the battery cables with a giant pair of shears.

"Along with a lot of bad air," said Bob. He put his hand on my shoulder. "It's just like when the dog dies. You gotta move on. Let's go see your new puppy."

The new puppy is a massive 1997 Dodge Ram that's been around the globe seven times. I prefer the simple boxy lines of the

Ford, but it seems everything they make is big and bulbous now. The Dodge does have cup holders and FM, innovations that were unknown in pickups in 1983. And it has a storage unit behind the seat, which is always handy in a farm truck.

It's just going to take some time.

House Guests

I grew up in a theatre family in Toronto in the 1950s when to claim you were an actor was tantamount to saying you were unemployed. My father was the only actor in the city who owned a house, and it came to be known as "The Club." For years, the third floor was a dormitory for actors "between successes" and our dinner table always stretched down into the shrubbery of the bay window to accommodate temporary guests. When we finally sold the house in 1977, my mother suggested to the new owners that they might want to change the locks because she had had hundreds of keys to the front door made over two decades. They didn't and three weeks later came downstairs to find an actor sleeping on the couch in the living room.

I eventually married into a farm family that belonged to the same tradition of easy hospitality. As a young man my father-in-law sailed the Atlantic seaboard on oil tankers and worked the coal mines, ranches and wheat fields of the west. His travels from those days brought many colourful characters back to the farm for indefinite stays. There was always room at their table for unexpected house guests. He would look up from his reading chair beside the wood stove when a strange car pulled into the yard and say, "Somebody on the highway heard your dinner bell, Mother."

When he passed away last summer in his seventy-eighth year, nearly four hundred people came to the farm to say farewell, some of them from great distances.

Here at Larkspur Farm there is a guest bedroom, couches and a couple of tents that stay pitched all summer. The habit of bringing home strays for dinner and sleepovers has found its way down to the third generation. My children, who have far stronger civic instincts than I ever did at their age, inherited their mother's facility for spotting people who need to be drawn into the warm circle of human contact on high holidays. In our house these would include Easter, Thanksgiving, professional development days, snow days, the annual rhubarb harvest . . . oh, and, of course, Christmas.

Writers are supposed to need absolute peace and quiet to function, and visitors often express amazement that I can form a coherent sentence with all the traffic that goes through this house. But I have always believed that a writer should live in the world as much as possible, and I find I work best when I can hear a happy hum of conversation down the hall in the kitchen or a spirited game of baseball on the front lawn.

Besides, I like feeding stuff—in the barn as well as the house. My wife says I handle the kids like fat sheep and brag to anyone who will listen about how much of the food on the table has been grown on the property. She doesn't get very excited about food miles, because she grew up on a farm where food delivery was measured in feet and inches and the menu never ventured further than beef, pork, potatoes and pie. To this day nothing gives her more pleasure than freighting in Meyer lemons from Israel or single-press olive oil from Tuscany. Together we create a balanced diet.

In my theatre family guests were prized for their exotic personalities and witty conversation. My wife's family admired any visitor who played an instrument and was willing to toss hay bales or vaccinate cattle. These two traditions merge here at Larkspur Farm. Our ideal house guest is someone who can snag a sheep, play the accordion, toss a stir-fry and perform scenes from *Monty*

Python and *The Goon Show*. But we'll settle for good conversation and help with the dishes.

The important thing is that this Christmas our dinner table will stretch out into the shrubbery of the bay window in our dining room. Each one of us will track down someone in the neighbourhood who for various reasons beyond their choosing has no one to share Christmas with. When the candles are lit and the children's faces shine in the light of a flaming pudding, we will count ourselves blessed.

The Farmer as Museum Piece

I took the family to the city for one of those mid-winter mental health excursions to visit the museum. On our way to the dinosaur exhibit we trooped past a group of exotic wild animals that have been displayed in various places around the building since I was a child. Rounding a corner, we came upon a new glass case containing a stuffed domestic chicken.

It was a very nice chicken, a showy white Leghorn rooster with a red comb, and it was certainly an appropriate specimen for those children who have no contact with barnyards or henhouses. But as a farmer I found it unsettling to see one of my own birds stuffed and soberly displayed beside cheetahs and pandas and other examples of the planet's vanishing wildlife. The desperate look in his glass eyes seemed to be shouting a warning that the curator and his taxidermist were coming for me next.

I live with a small flock of sheep and a henhouse down a blind road, about as far off the information highway as you can get. I chose this life a long time ago, trading in the fast lane for life on the off-ramp, a rural hamlet now rapidly being paved over and lit with sodium lights. In those days it was an hour-and-a-half drive north of the city. Progress has added a full hour to the trip. We still own a mailbox, dial phones, a private well and a septic tank. We remain off the grid for just about everything else, including natural gas, cable, pizza and *Globe and Mail* home delivery. Garbage pickup, dial-up and a satellite dish arrived only recently.

The old mixed farms around me have all vanished save one. Crashing prices for cattle and pigs have emptied the fields and barns of livestock, apart from a few flocks of sheep. Death Star–sized tractors and combines now visit the land for a few hours each spring and fall for planting and harvest, and on weekends frazzled urbanites head to neo-colonial ski chalets perched on the highest drumlin. I've been making jokes for years about how shepherds and skiers both have a tendency to die in debt, and I find it ironic that they appear to have inherited the earth in this neighbourhood.

Still, given the dwindling choices in our overscheduled world, it's a very nice place to live. The family farms of yesterday may be gone, but the families themselves are not. They're just doing something else. They still meet and connect in the same places—at the village diner, in the grocery store—and they still work on church committees and service clubs together. Many of the urban refugees are joining them in newly renovated community halls and recently founded arts and crafts groups. In some ways it's become a more interesting community with wider interests and occupations than it ever had when the grain elevators were the biggest building in town and the traditional meeting place was at the bottom of the escalator at Woolworth's.

There are even a few eccentrics like me who keep chickens and sheep. My next-door neighbour, a retired cattle farmer, has watched his children grow up and find occupations off the farm, but two of them still live next door to him. One farmhouse has been converted to a daycare centre and the other hosts a steel fabricating business. To his surprise two of his teenaged grandsons just established a new sheep flock. They filled a barn with crossbred ewes, and now the two of them zip down the road on a four-wheeler every morning to do chores before their school bus arrives. After all these years I finally have some company. The boys have joined my sheep committee at the fall fair and visit with me regularly to discuss mineral deficiencies and parasite control and other minutiae of the profession. No doubt their schooling will take them away from the Ninth Concession for a time, but I have a selfish reason for hoping they come back.

I won't feel so much like a candidate for that glass case at the museum.

My Failure as a Foodie

The agriculture I practise here at Larkspur Farm is neither organic nor particularly sustainable. In the great church of the whole food movement, I remain what I have always been, a stumbling Anglican in search of redemption.

My hens are not free-range; for their own protection they are allowed out only on the occasional supervised day pass. I haven't figured out how to keep livestock upright without vaccinations, dewormers and something that controls flies more consistently than a Muscovy duck. Grass-fed beef is a great concept on paper, but finding people who will eat the stuff is a different matter. People tell me it is possible to grow apples without chemical sprays; all you have to do is staple a plastic bag over each apple and vacuum the orchard every week.

I buy my livestock feed from Hamilton Brothers farm supply down in Glen Huron, an establishment most food purists would classify as a vertically integrated agribusiness conglomerate and a place of sin. Although it doesn't appear to me to be all that integrated when Ted the miller is on lunch and I'm tripping over cat dishes in the back of the mill trying to find a bag of mixed grain.

So it comes as a huge relief to hear from one of the high priests of food that anyone who grows and eats their own food is basically on the right track. Michael Pollan, the author of *The Omnivore's Dilemma* and *In Defense of Food*, says that we are making ourselves sick because we eat food products instead of real food. He has just issued a ringing manifesto: "Eat food. Not too much. Mostly plants." Pollan claims that science has failed us by launching a flurry of high-fibre, low-cholesterol, omega-3-rich, sodium-reduced confections onto the market and it is high time we handed the job of feeding people back to local culture. He suggests that we avoid eating food that comes in a box or a pouch, pay more attention to where it comes from and stop obsessing about whether it's grown organically or conventionally. Nothing less than our lives depends on it.

"We stand at a fork in the road," he says. "We're either going to get used to chronic disease . . . or we're going to change the way we eat."

Just sitting down to a meal with my children is like attending a political rally. Vegetarians, fair traders, anti-globalists, slow foodies and health faddists surround me. The only groups not represented are the weed-choppers and the bale-tossers, whose activities have been targeted by a local campaign to stamp out child labour.

The fact is, my reading has not convinced me there is any persuasive scientific evidence that organic anything offers any clear advantage over its conventional counterpart, especially if it has been trucked all the way from California. But I hardly need to consult a book to see how our industrial approach to food production is destroying the health of land, animals and human communities everywhere. I sometimes wish I had my children's messianic certainty about these issues, but the older I get, the more I am struck by just how little we know about the complexity of the human body and the way it reacts to the natural world.

"You're just like Socrates, Pop," chirps my son, the rock guitarist and duck hunter who now abjures dairy products. "You know nothing except the fact of your ignorance."

"Which is the beginning of wisdom, little grasshopper," I reply gravely. "Now eat your carrots."

Duck Soup

J ust got back from the first day of the spring duck hunt, which opened this morning with an excursion to the swamps of Grey County.

This should not be confused with the fall duck hunt, which is supervised by the Ministry of Natural Resources. Our spring duck hunt is supervised by my eleven-year-old daughter, Hannah, and it takes us to venues across southwestern Ontario in search of exotic domesticated bird species to repopulate the farm for the summer. Winter takes its toll on all of us. Duck fever strikes every year as the snow melts and continues till the season closes, usually by July 1, when my wife says, "Enough ducks!"

Our hunt is not restricted to just ducks. We'll take guinea hens, chukar partidges, Polish mop head chickens or just about anything except for Muscovy ducks, which we find too crabby, or any goose that the two of us cannot lift. Sometimes, we get sidetracked and come home with a rabbit or a goldfish.

Hannah has been a poultry fancier since the age of four when our Chinese gander made the mistake of sneaking up on her and biting her on the bum. She whirled around, grabbed him by the throat and strained him through the page-wire gate. Then she climbed over the gate and chased him all the way down to the pond with a hockey stick. The gander always kept a respectful distance after that, warning his harem, "Don't go near the pink one. She's got a club."

Hannah's Rule has always been "Never Back Away from Poultry," a principle she applies to other subjects besides birds.

I love rainy spring days in auction barns, listening to the patter of an auctioneer and munching a peameal bacon sandwich. Today we are looking for white Pekin ducks at the Keady Livestock Market auction, which has been held in the same place every Tuesday morning at ten o'clock sharp since about 1953.

There are no white ducks on offer today, but we take a fancy to the very last lot of the sale, a box of pretty-coloured Silkie hens, and we bid them all the way up to three dollars apiece. The auctioneer and owner, Ron Kuhl, solemnly knocks them down to us and smiles when he sees Hannah.

"It's a good idea to get them started young," he says.

I tell him how another Ron got me hooked on poultry many years ago, when I was thirteen. He was a livestock dealer on a farm up the road from us, who hired me for a dollar an hour every summer to bring in hay. On Thursday mornings, before dawn, he would pick me up and drive down to the Kitchener sales barns where he bought cattle, sheep and pigs. One day I noticed that pigeons were trading in Kitchener for seventy-five cents apiece. There were hundreds of pigeons in the barns back home, so that night I tied a feed sack around my neck, climbed to the peak of the haymow and went hand over hand along the hay-track, feeling gingerly for little pigeon feet. I snagged fifty the first week, packed them in a crate and doubled my wages with a Thursday delivery to Kitchener.

Ron's eyebrows shot up as he listened to my story. "You know, I did exactly the same thing," he laughs.

But he had a bad experience that ended the enterprise. "I was working my way down the track one night grabbing pigeons," he recalls. "And I put my hand on one and it turned out to be a little barn owl."

Ouch! That was it for Ron's midnight pigeon hunts. In my case, I simply wiped out the local population and had to turn to raising rabbits and fancy chickens for extra cash. But I was hooked for life. Today Hannah cradles the box on her lap and names each chicken as it pokes its head up through the flaps: Charlotte, Emily, Henrietta and Olive. She's hooked too.

Next Saturday we're off to the Mount Forest Fur and Feather Show. There's sure to be a white duck there.

A Seven-Step Program to
Getting Horse Free

S **tep 1. Face the music.**
First you have to admit there's a problem. You bought the horse years ago for a ten-year-old daughter who swore she would brush it every day and lavish it with affection. That was before she discovered boys, clothes, makeup and Facebook. Now the horse stands in the pasture swatting flies with a companion horse and two other visiting horses that were dumped off by your daughter's friends before they went off to jobs with merchant banks.

Each year these horses munch through ten tons of hay and convert it to another ten tons of manure, all of which has to be shovelled by hand. Each animal suffers an expensive ailment that periodically brings the vet to your door with another soul-crushing prescription. You ask hopefully if the diagnosis is terminal, but he just grins. "Nothing lives longer than a horse with a health problem!" he says as he purrs out the lane in his Land Rover.

Step 2. Imagine the freedom.

In economics the term "opportunity cost" is used to help people visualize all the things they might otherwise be doing with an investment that is not working out. Try to look at it this way: owning a pleasure horse is like not having a two-week time-share in a Tuscan villa or not staying at the Park Hyatt pretty much whenever you like.

Step 3. Cancel all horse magazine subscriptions.

After all these years with horses, your mailbox is stuffed full of magazines and flyers that offer great deals on high-tensile fencing, red-oak stabling, compact tractors, organic supplements, copper weather vanes and whispering seminars on "How to Cure the Problem Horse." These pirates have ripped a gaping hole in the side of your household ship, and now you must start throwing freight overboard.

Step 4. Stop hanging around horse people.

Avoid people with British fox-hunting prints on the wall and three decompression chambers between the barn and the broadloom. Such people have lantern jaws, gin veins on the nose and voices that hang on the air like hoof paint. They talk all night about stud books and trips to Lexington, and you stagger away from their dinner parties with exactly the same feeling you get on the way back from the city, that is, that you aren't making enough money or having as much fun as everybody else.

Step 5. Be prepared to tell a little white lie.

"She's a dear old thing." "Just loves children." "Absolutely no vices." Mother warned us what happened to little children who tell lies. But God will forgive you, apparently, because he has been turning a blind eye to the things that horse people say since Roman times. In fact, it was the horse deal that gave us the ancient legal concept of *caveat emptor*. What you see is what you get. Besides, did anybody tell you anything approaching the truth about this horse when they sold it to you? Didn't it come as a bit of a surprise when it ate all the boards off the barn?

Step 6. Prepare to take a bath.
Think of your absolutely rock-bottom, lowest price and then cut it in half. This will sting a bit, but soon you will be rewarded with that light, springy sensation that horses get when the saddle and bridle come off and they are released into a lush pasture . ▼ . forever.

If any offer is made, take it. Remember, the selling prices in the horse magazines and on the notice board in the tack shop are pure fiction, like the conversations between Ginger and Black Beauty. Unless some innocent like you comes along to upset the market, a horse usually trades for a snowmobile of the same vintage or a set of snow tires.

Step 7. Plow the fields with salt.
Tear down the fences; chop the farm into cottage lots; set fire to the barn; report yourself to the Humane Society. Every morning, stand in front of the mirror and say, "I am a recovering horse person. I will never take another horse, even as a gift."

One Lucky Turkey

C ountry properties have been a dumping ground for unwanted animals since ancient times. The Roman orator Cicero complained in a letter to his wife about a visitor to his country villa who left a difficult dog with him and wouldn't come back to pick it up.

It's not just the problem dogs from the city and the chicks from the school incubation project that find their way into our hearts and my office. The farmers themselves have found our place a convenient one to offload farm animals at the end of their rope or the bottom of their economic cycle. We continually find ourselves with bottle-fed lambs, old cows, runty pigs, foundered horses and pensioned goats.

So it came as no surprise when I came home one day last spring and found my eleven-year-old daughter cradling a three-day-old turkey chick that had been dropped off by one of the neighbours, a young woman who raises a thousand turkeys every year for city restaurants. It was a startling shade of pink.

"They spray them with a pink dye at the hatchery as they're being vaccinated," she explained. "This one went through the sprayer three times. Isn't she the sweetest thing?"

Hannah decided to call her Candy Floss and put her in a cage on the floor of my office.

"Great," I said. "And what sort of future do you think she has?" Turkey chicks are famously fragile and expire at the drop of a hat. Even if they do survive to adulthood, the White Rocks are designed to put on weight so fast that their cardiopulmonary systems can't keep up. Sparing a turkey from Thanksgiving dinner just means it will succumb to "flipover" disease a few months later. This is the technical term that poultry people use to describe a turkey heart attack. There could be no happy outcome to this project. As a pet, Candy Floss was strapped into a handcar on a set of tracks leading straight off a cliff.

Hannah didn't hear a word I said, of course. Within a week Candy Floss was trotting around behind her like a devoted dog, charming visitors with her gentle trilling and posing for photographs. Not surprisingly this did not sit well with our Cairn terrier, Haggis, who is a jealous dog and will have no other dogs before him. He has murdered two lovebirds and a couple of ducks in his career, and there were several close calls. For the next two months Candy Floss moved around the farm like the blind Magoo in the old cartoon, happily oblivious to the threats made on her life. She required a constant bodyguard. Cats hung in the branches of the cherry tree above her, tails twitching. A turkey vulture circled ominously in the late afternoons. Haggis lay each night beside her cage, quietly plotting.

We put Candy Floss on a low-protein diet of Irish steel-cut oats that she still takes in a bowl with us every morning at breakfast. In the evening we encouraged her to forage for greens and bugs in the sheep pasture. Hannah discovered that she just loves a handful of the live crickets she feeds to her gecko. But crickets cost ten cents each and buying enough to support an adult turkey's cricket habit would be like taking out a second mortgage. Financial ruin was narrowly averted by a wet summer that produced a bumper crop of free local crickets. Then I put my back out turning stones to find them for her.

If a bird can survive on love alone, Candy Floss should live forever. Her weight is still a concern. Even on a diet of crickets and oats she tipped the scales at ten pounds by the end of the summer. It looks like we will have a turkey for Thanksgiving dinner as we always do, but this year she will be sitting at the table with us and I think we will be serving a smoked ham.

A Friend in the Garden

Once again the clamour from the federal election has put me in an ill humour, and my wife has sent me out to the garden by the fish pond with an old friend who always helps me make sense of the world. This particular pal has been dead for over four centuries, but his voice is just as fresh and amusing as it was when I first stumbled into his company, nearly forty years ago.

My grandfather put the works of Michel de Montaigne into my hands at Christmastime when I was in my last year of high school. He had been felled by a stroke and was distributing his enormous library among his grandchildren when I appeared at his bedside in dirty jeans fresh from moving my fat pigs to the packing house.

"Of the thirteen grandchildren, I thought you were the one that should have these," he said gravely, handing me an ancient cloth-bound volume of Montaigne's *Essais*, together with a copy of Thoreau's *Walden* and a collection of E.B. White's writings from *The New Yorker*. "They have all been good friends to me and if you are going to spend much more time out there on your mother's wretched farm, you will need all the friends you can get. All of these writers were escape artists just like you." And he patted the books affectionately in farewell.

Like my grandfather and me, Montaigne bolted from the city in mid-career to make a home in the boonies where he could write, reflect and grow his own vegetables. Through the title of his book *Essais*, a term he coined to describe his attempts to come to a formal understanding of some difficult subject, he gave us the English word "essay."

His motto, "What do I know?" was the product of twenty years' experience mediating between murderous factions during the religious wars of sixteenth-century France. His was a voice of moderation and gentle skepticism in an era famous for its fanaticism and intolerance. An advisor to kings, Montaigne probably fed Henry IV that famous line about making sure every worker had a chicken in the pot for Sunday dinner. But the work discouraged and disgusted Montaigne so severely that he made up his mind to devote the rest of his life to serious study, the enjoyment of life's pleasures and the preparation of his mind for death, which came fairly early for him, at age fifty-nine. Unlike many of his friends who fell to the assassin's blade in the mean streets of Paris, he died peacefully in his bed in his farmhouse in the Dordogne.

When Montaigne announced his decision to move out of town, his friends were horrified and asked how he would survive in the lawless countryside without men-at-arms and a fortified house. He replied that the trick to survival was to live simply and make it look like you have nothing worth taking. He suffered only one serious misadventure and that was due to a fall from a horse in heavy traffic in Paris, an experience he described in clinical detail in an essay that should be glued to every saddle today, like the warning labels on tractors and wood chippers.

"Ambition is never better directed than by a straying and unfrequented path," he insisted. His sole ambition by that time was to come to a better understanding of a chaotic, dangerous, but still beautiful world. Everything was literary fodder to him, whether he was yanking an onion out of the ground or musing about the futility of trying to be a king. And when he was strolling through his orchard observing the meanderings of a beetle, the ground would open up beneath him and he could see straight through to the centre of the earth.

"I want death to find me planting my cabbages, but caring little about it, and even less for my imperfect garden."

I am embarrassed to say that the edition of *Essais* my grandfather gave me that Christmas went missing years ago and has had to be replaced twice. This is what comes of reading in gardens. But my wife keeps track of my old friends better than I do and at Christmas often sees that they are restored to me.

Emergency Measures

L ast fall my wife and I flew to England to spend a week with an old friend who lives on a farm in south Devon. On the plane somewhere over the Atlantic in the middle of the night, Heath suffered a heart attack. She lay on the floor of the plane for three hours until we finally landed at Gatwick. A waiting ambulance rushed her to the East Surrey hospital where surgeons performed an angiogram, installed a stent and ordered five days of bed rest in the cardiac ward. It was quite a shock, considering she was only forty-six and had been given no reason to be worried about her health.

On the bright side, we were given excellent care by the British hospital staff and Heath is expected eventually to make a full recovery. And the experience reminded me once again how brilliant a small rural community can be at handling a crisis.

I have always found that, compared with their city cousins, country people respond to calamity much differently. They don't send a card wishing you well or call after a couple of days and say, "If there's anything I can do, please let us know." They drive straight over as soon as they hear the sirens or see the smoke or pick up the news at any one of thirty-two outlets for public information in the neighbourhood. And they always do something useful.

Heath is related to everyone between Highway 9 and Georgian Bay. I knew that within minutes of my initial call home, her mother and sisters would be heading for our house, spreading the news by cell phone. By noon the first neighbour would be on the veranda with food, offering to take the kids for a night, run a vacuum cleaner or take a shift doing chores in my barn. By the time I eventually did get home, I knew my biggest job would be to return all the casserole dishes and pie plates to their owners. If the authorities ever want to study up on how to improve the quality of their emergency measure techniques, they should watch a rural community in action. The efficiency is breathtaking.

When the doctors declared Heath out of danger, they advised her not to fly for at least two weeks and suggested we find a quiet place to convalesce. So I called our friend in Devon and told her it might be best to postpone our visit until another occasion when Heath was feeling better.

"Nonsense," said Philippa, who has always spoken to me like an elder sister. "You came all this way to stay with me! Come down here right away!"

As soon as we arrived at her farm in the tiny hamlet of Copplestone, a few miles from Dartmoor, we were quickly absorbed into the life of a small English village. More pies and casseroles appeared at the door. A car was put at our disposal. Dinner invitations came over the telephone. When Heath ventured out for a walk, we invariably got only a few hundred feet before a door opened and we were invited in for tea. One of the neighbours turned out to be related to a family just down the road from us back in Canada, although the cousins hadn't actually been in touch since about 1840.

"Why don't they ever write?" the man asked with a grin.

One dark night we got hopelessly lost in the spiderweb of country lanes on the way to a dinner party. I finally stopped at a crossroads and opened the door of a crowded village pub to ask directions.

"Could anyone tell me how to get to Ben Gray's farm?" I said in a loud voice. The room fell silent for a moment, and the patrons all shook their heads.

"It's too complicated," said the publican, handing me a cell phone. "You'd be better off to call him and he'll drive down and lead you up to the farm. What's Ben's number?" he called over his shoulder. A man with a dart in one hand and a pint in the other called back without looking away from the dartboard.

"1316 2478! Are you the Canadians? She's feeling better now is she?"

All very much like home on the Ninth Concession.

A Bridge of Sighs

I t's not a pretty structure and has next to no historical significance, except that people have been crossing the Pretty River in
that place for nearly two hundred years. It's a single-lane concrete
bridge that the local government built in 1932, at the height of the
Depression. Call it Nottawasaga Township's statement of faith in
the future, a stimulus package of the day for the cash-strapped
farmers of the Back Settlement. Many of them teamed wagons
full of gravel and stone up the Tenth Concession to help with the
construction and received a much-needed credit on their property
taxes in return. It took about a month to build and cost fifteen
hundred dollars. It served the community for twenty-five years
until a storm washed it out in 1957 and a faithful replica was built,
again with a lot of local labour.

But now it fails to meet the specifications for a modern bridge
and is slated for replacement. We should be grateful that our
governments have found seven hundred thousand dollars to do
the job. But this month when the provincial freshwater fish czar
finally signs off on the project and the bulldozers move into the
streambed, I will feel a twinge of regret.

I call it the Civility Bridge because it has an uncanny way of
separating the human population into two groups: those with

manners and those with none. The drivers of two cars approaching from either direction can see each other from over half a mile away. By their relative positions and rates of travel, they have plenty of time to judge which car will get to the bridge first, unless, of course, the rate of speed of one car changes abruptly. You can tell almost instantly whether the person in the other car is a local or a weekender by the way he or she approaches that bridge. Generally a local person will take his foot off the gas and coast to the bridge, looking for a signal from the other driver that it is safe to proceed. People "from away" are more likely to goose it as soon as they see opposition on the horizon and zip over the bridge at sixty miles an hour.

This can be hazardous, and the bridge bears many scars. A lot of mirrors lie broken on the roadbed. The simple concrete fence pattern is frayed and spiderwebbed with cracks from the blows and sideswipes it has taken over the years. In several places you can see the reinforcing steel exposed and rusting.

It's not that the locals are an angelic and deferential people. On the contrary, they can be as competitive and hot-tempered as any hedge fund manager or tax lawyer from the city. It's just that a local knows that when he stomps on the gas and roars over the bridge, he is very likely to catch a glimpse of the face in the other windshield, and it will turn out that he has just cut off Helen McLeod, a sweet-faced grandmother of four and the lady who dropped in last month to give him a jar of her homemade mustard pickle. And this makes him look like an oaf, which is just exactly what he is. It is the same hesitation that strikes any of us before we honk the horn in the Loblaws parking lot. Because we know our next words may be, "Oh, pardon me, vicar!"

When Civility Bridge is gone, the last remnant of decorum on the Tenth Concession will go with it. When I first moved up here thirty years ago and the Tenth was still a gravel road, I remember every driver you passed here offered at least a wave and, on occasion, pulled to a stop, rolled down the window and asked if you needed a ticket to the fair board beef dinner fundraiser.

I suppose we need the stimulus, although economists today tend to agree that infrastructure money never trickles down to the pockets of those who need it, the way it did in the low-tech days of the Hoover Dam and the Tennessee Valley Authority. They say the bulk of the money flows into the hands of consultants and foreign equipment manufacturers. Still, seven hundred thousand dollars is a lot of cash and, if past experience is anything to go by, the project will provide at least eight months of sport for an army of engineers, planners, stream consultants, fish doctors, attendant lords, heralds, minstrels and mutes-on-foot.

Rhonda's diner down in the village should have a good year.

Spreading Affection

I have worked on a personal computer every morning for the last thirty years, but I have never grown to like the damn thing. I should say "things," for there have been about seven over that time, each one faster than the one before. These advances have been pretty much wasted on me, because I don't think or type any faster than I did when I was twenty-five. I follow the same ant track and punch all the same keys I always did, unless, of course, the machine starts to flash a "system error." Then I take it to the store where the twelve-year-old behind the counter tells me the machine has become hopelessly outdated and must be replaced.

Out in the barn it's a different matter. There I have gathered a collection of tools and machines for which I feel considerable affection. They each perform only one task, unlike a personal computer that tries to do everything. But the barn machines do their one task reliably and well. They are inexpensive and durable, and most are second-hand. Any person of ordinary intelligence can repair them. And when I use them, they do not disrupt anything good about the farm, or my family or the neighbourhood.

Take my manure spreader, for example. It's an Oliver Cockshutt 471, built in 1959 in Brantford, Ontario, and shipped by train to the Hamilton Brothers farm supply in Glen Huron, where it was purchased by my neighbours, the Currie brothers, and put to work in their dairy barn for three decades until I bought it at their auction sale in 1989. Since then it has been a source of endless novelty for me. It sports many of the same simple mechanical actions that gave us the Industrial Revolution and drove our ancestors across the Atlantic to the forests of Upper Canada. It has a gearbox, a worm-drive gear, a pitman shaft, a ratchet gear, several roller chains, a slip-clutch and any number of bearings, sprockets and pulleys. Everything except the deck and sides is made of cast or chilled steel. When the power take-off lever is engaged, it clatters to life with a heart-stopping noise something like baseball-sized hail landing on a steel roof, but its triple beaters lay down manure like a broadloom carpet. Dandelions cheer when it goes by.

It is surprisingly reliable for its age and never dull. When this machine spits up a system error message, you tend to remember the moment for the rest of your natural life. I have learned to start it very gently in freezing weather, and I usually wear a hard hat and a thick coat because it throws stones. Once I fired it up without realizing a ball of yellow jackets had made a home on the middle beater. I escaped in fourth gear but took the corner boards off the barn in the process. The latest Cockshutt moment occurred just recently while I was spreading pig poop in the field behind the house. Suddenly the apron chain jammed on an old crowbar that had somehow found its way into the manure pile. I lunged for the PTO lever but too late. The cast-iron dog on the pitman gear snapped and left the beaters flailing helplessly.

As I stood on the gunwales in my tennis shoes in the stifling heat, forking the load off piece by piece, I should have been upset or even furious at the inconvenience. But I was not. I thought of the relics of the Information Age that have failed me in the past— the laser printer, the espresso machine, the VCR—and I figured living well is the best revenge after all. Cast steel can be welded. I will bond more deeply with the spreader as I pull it apart and put it back together. Fodder for breakfast conversation down at the diner with the Currie brothers.

The Cockshutt will live to fight another day.

Two Men on a Roof

I am about to put new red steel on the roof of our little sheep barn. I have been joined in this effort by my fourteen-year-old son, Matthew, who has a strong personal interest in the project. The roof has just lately started to leak above the workbench in the upstairs modelling room where he paints his soldiers.

My mother used to say that all roofers were drunks. She could be forgiven that blind prejudice in Mono Township in the 1960s, because it seemed that no one ever climbed up on a roof in that community without a case of beer. Every second man in the neighbourhood limped from a fall and more than one had been struck by lightning.

The roofer I spent the most time with was Russell "Honey" Thompson, a Baptist beekeeper from Mono Centre who never touched a drop (if you didn't count the tumbler of dandelion wine he drank every morning for breakfast). Russell and his partner, Albert Foster, worked for half a century together, building barns and drive sheds all over Dufferin County in southern Ontario. Russell joked that they stuck together because Albert was right-handed and Russell was left-handed, which meant they never had to argue about which end of the roof they would shingle. But the real reason I suspect had more to do with the conversation between them. It was a pretty one-sided chat. Russell was probably the best storyteller the township ever produced. Fortunately Albert was one of the great listeners of his time. People said that once you got Albert Foster started listening, it was hard to get him stopped.

I mentioned my mother's opinion of roofers to Russell once while he was supervising the installation of steel sheeting on our new calf barn in 1968. This prompted a morning's worth of stories about drunk roofers, drunk dentists and drunk chickens. Just before lunch Russell paused and said he believed that it was unwise for a person to work on a roof alone, as much because of the physical risks as the mental ones. Russell was an authority on the rhythm and the pace of work. He said that two men look out for each other on a roof and tend to make better decisions together than they would on their own.

"There are worse things you can do for a friendship than to spend the day looking out for each other," he said.

Today Matthew is looking out for me as we erect rented scaffolding up to the eavestrough. Russell would have scoffed at the expense wasted on this foolishness. "Scaffolding just makes you flip once before you hit the ground," he would say. "Tie a rope on yourself and learn to walk on the nails." And then he would tell the story about the time he hauled a ladder up onto the steep roof of the house to give him a better footing while cleaning the chimney. To secure the ladder he tossed a rope over the peak and tied it to the bumper of his truck. Then his wife Daisy came out, got in the truck and drove off to town. The ladder went up over the peak like a javelin and snagged on the mailbox at the end of the lane, leaving Russell stranded on the roof until Daisy returned at suppertime, fifty feet of rope still trailing behind the truck.

But Matthew knows that a writer should always have a rope on him and scaffolding behind him, especially one who already limps and whose thoughts wander from the task at hand as much as mine do. We are both right-handers, and it is touching to hear him say, "Stay put, old man," as he moves around me to nail the strapping at the left edge.

The Benedictine monks told us that work is prayer. The poet Wendell Berry says that work is a dance. Today, with a breeze in our hair and a commanding view of the farms of the Back Settlement, it is a conversation, and one of which Russell would have approved.

The Larkspur Supper Club

C hristmas entertaining here at Larkspur Farm is becoming less about presents and more about food. Instead of driving to the mall, we're more likely to head downstairs to the freezer for a couple of roasts and throw together another dinner party.

When you have a farm that is stocked with sheep, pigs, cows, chickens, four children and all their pets, your friends gradually come around to the fact that it's just easier if they come to you. We have a kitchen that joins onto a dining room that spills out onto a veranda and a big front yard. The screen door swings so often the hinges have to be replaced every couple of years. All through the year most Saturday evenings draw a group of regulars to an informal banquet we call the Larkspur Supper Club.

The group is elastic and can expand to include twenty-five adults and children drawn from city and country. We have a butcher, a baker, a candlestick maker, a couple of farmers, a teacher, an actor and two big-city entrepreneurs. All of us like to eat good food and visit far into the night.

When I was growing up, the rules of etiquette decreed that likes and dislikes were not appropriate dinner conversation. But at the Larkspur Supper Club, we inevitably drift back to the same subject: the food we like best and how it should make its way to our table. What I love about this conversation is the way the cooks, the farmers and the butcher exchange information. They puzzle and worry and debate about the ideal pasture-hut chicken or the correct time to pick a pear. Then they sit down and sample the chicken and the pear as if my house is a test kitchen.

Every time I pick up a food magazine, I get the impression that butchers and bakers and farmers all inhabit their own silos and seldom talk to one another. It's like the carpenters, plasterers and electricians who put the addition on my house years ago. Each trade blamed the other for delays and mistakes, and by the end of the project I wanted to send them all on a three-day conference to figure out how a house should be built.

A lot of cooks know everything about preparing food but virtu-ally nothing about farming. The opposite is also true. The art of the butcher is a mystery to almost everyone. Many cooks are surprised to learn that fresh, free-range eggs are not available in most of Canada in winter because hens stop laying when it's cold and dark. But despite that gap in their understanding, the cooks can still join a discussion about the compromises we make to persuade a Canadian hen to lay an egg in February. Both the farmer and the chef may be surprised to learn from the butcher how the fat cover on a carcass determines the length of time meat can be aged. And the butcher could learn a thing or two from the inventiveness of a cook who has found a new way to present pork belly. Of course, it certainly helps if the people involved actually enjoy one another's company, have a glass of wine in hand and don't feel that they must have the final word on the subject of food.

This is a conversation that is taken for granted in Italy and France and many other parts of the world. I recently had a fairly pointed reminder of why it's high time we took it up in earnest here in North America. One day this summer I was giving a group of small children a tour of the farm and at the end handed each of them an egg fresh out of the henhouse.

"Oh no," protested a seven-year-old in horror. "I don't want an egg that comes from a chicken."

Every screen in the house and on the street has already begun to proclaim the Christmas message of peace and good will. For our part, we will be doubling up on our meetings of the Larkspur Supper Club, debating and wrangling far into the night, searching for the ideal way to finish a beef or smoke a turkey.

Chances are we will find harmony in all of this.

Weather Signs

M y friends in the city always look to me each year for some clue about the kind of winter we're going to get. They assume that because I live out here on the farm so close to nature, I can tell if there is an extra layer of moss on the north side of the cedar trees or how deep the frogs have dug into the bottom of the pond.

Of course, I don't do any of that. Because I studied economics, I do have formal training in how to make incorrect predictions. But when baling hay I check with the drones at the weather office, the same as my city friends do before a game of golf. I used to consult a few genuine oracles, but they are disappearing as the culture gives way to satellite imagery and hand-held devices.

My wife's dad was a sailor, a shepherd and a weather sage. He was plugged into an enormous database of bizarre Celtic incantations that offered a rhyming couplet for all seasons. It was sort of like Hallmark cards for Druids.

There were the usual ones about taking warning from a red sky in morning or making the connection between mares' tails and short sails. He would step out on the front stoop, pause and squint at a pale moon, and say cryptically, "There's water in her eye," which meant rain when you didn't want it. Or he might glance up at the chimney and declare, "When smoke descends fair weather ends." Sometimes he would glare at birds in the fields and mutter, "Seagulls on the sand," which I didn't learn till years later was one half of a dark observation about gulls coming to the land whenever a storm threatened at sea. This is still puzzling, because there are seagulls sitting out in my field today, just where they have been on every pleasant sunny day for the past thirty years.

None of these observations ever offered happy news about the weather. I once asked my father-in-law what two rings around the sun meant, and his dour reply was: "Basically crap weather for the next six months." Squeaky chairs, catchy drawers and sticky salt all worked together to reinforce that message.

Father has been gone for two years now, but my fifteen-year-old son has inherited his zest for gloomy views into the future. He just came back from the latest doomsday film *2012*, which is the year the ancient Mayan calendar comes to an end and the world with it, in hi-def, slo-mo devastation.

My friend the classics scholar tells me that the Mayan calendar does indeed come to an end in 2012, but then it just resets to zero, like the odometer on my old farm truck. Not that I want to be reminded of the day that happened. What a catastrophe it was. We were coming up the Ninth Concession from the mailbox, all hunched over and staring at the instrument panel as the row of nines clicked over to zeroes. We cheered, and I turned into the lane and promptly ran over Daffy Duck. The cheers turned to weeping and wailing and gnashing of teeth, not one stone was left upon another and several fingers were pointed. But after a while things settled down, I buried the duck and things went back to normal as they always do.

It was a surreal moment, because Daffy Duck had been something of a doomsday figure herself. She was a scruffy Rouen who led a monastic life, brooding on her nest under a bench in the stable for months on end, eating nothing and muttering darkly. Then suddenly, mid-June, she would burst out into the yard, quacking at the air like some crazy person you might see walking erratically on a downtown street. We called her Daffy "The Sky Is

Falling" Duck and tried to make sense of her dire predictions. It turned out she was right all along, but judging from her startled expression when the final cataclysm came, it caught her completely unprepared.

"Dad, if the Mayans were able to see a thousand years into the future, shouldn't they have seen the Spanish coming?" asked my son.

A good point, I thought. As Shakespeare told us, it isn't much help knowing what is to come. The readiness is all. With that in mind, I have three bush cords of maple stacked against the house and a stack of poultry magazines to wade through between potluck suppers, film club nights and crop outlook seminars at the Co-op.

And, of course, the odd trip south to a hotel in the city.

Appearing Nightly

About twenty years ago, when my first book came out, I was invited to do a reading at a writers' luncheon in Ottawa. I was terribly nervous about taking my barnyard stories in front of a serious literary crowd, and I spent a sleepless night in the hotel beforehand. At the lunch I sat beside one of my heroes, the diarist Charles Ritchie, who was then in his mid-eighties, suffering from an abscessed tooth and not very interested in conversation. But when my turn came at the podium, the audience responded warmly to my stories of the old farm community and gave me an enthusiastic ovation.

When I sat down, Ritchie leaned over to me and patted my hand admiringly. "You're a hit, dear boy," he said. "A palpable hit!"

That lunch placed me firmly on the speaking circuit. Since then, I have never been more than a week or two away from some platform in the hinterland. I am not an A-list speaker; you will not find me in big-city hotel banquet rooms. My work takes me more often to Legion halls, Best Western dining rooms, hockey arenas, auction barns and beef barbecue picnics.

My skills are sorely tested at times. I have struggled with terrible sound systems, shrieking babies, smashing plates in the kitchen, a bagpiper circling outside the tent, roars from the crowd of two thousand people watching a midget toss in the building next door. Never, ever go up against a midget toss.

At the Sheep and Wool Fair at the arena in Markdale, Ontario, I tried to address a crowd jammed into the bleachers surrounding an acre of sheep in pens. I stood on the auction platform in the middle and every time I told a joke and the crowd laughed, the sheep would start to baa. When I suggested to the audience that they try to enjoy the humour inwardly, they burst out laughing and set the sheep off again.

I once competed at a farm bankers' convention with two televisions playing the World Series at the back of the hall. I appeared at one very late-season outdoor barbecue with snow whirling through the crowd. I nearly left the profession after playing to a dead-silent Mennonite Christmas party. (But I was heartened when their leader called me to say that everyone had had a wonderful time and would I come back again?)

Farm meetings traditionally take place in the worst weather and are never cancelled. I have crawled through blizzards and worked around police roadblocks, knowing that even nuclear winter would not interrupt a soil and crop meeting. We live in our own private snow globe here on Georgian Bay, and usually the trick is just to get out of our valley and find out what the weather is doing that day in the rest of Ontario. My winter driving checklist includes snow tires, insulated shoes, a spare shirt (in case of turkey gravy accidents) and lately, over my protests, a cell phone. But I don't need any entertainment devices in the car. My kids laugh because for ten years I carried only one tape in my ancient Camry, a scratchy copy of the soundtrack to *The Commitments*. Sometimes on the long drive home I might listen to CBC's *Ideas* or some far-off baseball game. But for the last hour and a half across the frozen steppes of Grey County, I usually drive in blissful silence.

As a writer, I count myself blessed because I like my audience. I like sitting at long, folding tables piled with grey roast beef, steamed peas and mashed potatoes and visiting with people for whom visiting is an essential part of life. I share their wintry sense of humour and their love of war stories from the farm.

After twenty years and nearly a thousand speeches, I sometimes wonder if perhaps it isn't time to fold up my travelling podium and call it quits. I find it hard to get to sleep if I'm not home in my own bed. But then the phone rings and a lovely voice asks me if I'm free for the fiftieth anniversary of the Holstein Club Ladies Night next November, and my wife looks at me and smiles. "Well, you gotta do that."

A Charter Case for Chickens

Out here on the Ninth Concession we are free to do any number of things that are forbidden in town. We can still start a bonfire, allow a dog to run loose, dig a well, park three cars on the lawn, play loud music, fire weapons into the hill and keep chickens without a permit.

Of course, we pay a price for these freedoms. The road into town is a bone-rattling affair that shakes our vehicles into early graves. It has been patched every year since I moved here in 1978, but it has never received an end-to-end coating of gravel in living memory. We are often trapped down our blind line for several days in winter, and the underground phone cables and switches have frozen and thawed so many times that we now sound like some of the older residents, shouting into the phone as if the listener is standing on the other side of a plowed field. But these are minor irritations compared with the luxury of maintaining our charter right to hear a mourning dove or a morning rooster.

Apparently I am not the only one to notice this difference between city and country freedoms. According to a CBC radio program I was listening to last month, a number of urban groups are getting up on their hind legs and pushing hard to get municipal councils to repeal bylaws that prohibit backyard chicken flocks.

Raising food is a basic human right, they say, guaranteed in the United Nations Declaration of 1947, and they quote heavy hitters from Solon to Seneca to support their case. I was listening to this debate on the very day I was installing a hundred meat chicks in the two pasture huts I keep out behind the house. And it was a debate, because two people called in to oppose the idea for every voice raised in support.

I think the activists are going about it the wrong way. These days if you tell the authorities what you think you have the right to do and try to change a bylaw, you just alert all the unemployed know-nothings and nattering nannies who have the time to march down to city hall with a placard to oppose your suggestion and recommend two new bylaws to regulate fish tanks and bird-cages. The Russians learned many wars ago to ignore the state's pronouncements on food production, because the consequences of food insecurity were too awful to contemplate. The Russian backyard remains the most reliable source of food for that nation to this day.

But our nation is stirring. A nerve has been plucked. Agitators from Lac du Bonnet to Windsor and Calgary to Toronto are stock-piling illegal eggs from their backyard grow-ops to pelt at city hall. "Aux armes, citoyens!" they cry. "Solidarity with the sideroads." And I will be happy to join them on the barricades.

The City of Guelph, Ontario, is a haven of common sense on this subject. It has a chicken bylaw that hasn't been changed since 1947 and has no intention of messing with it. The law allows backyard flocks as long as they are confined and set back a minimum distance of fifty feet from a dwelling. The authorities have no problem with roosters, because roosters are a noise problem, which comes under the jurisdiction of the police. Most normal people are too embarrassed to call the police about a rooster, and even elderly officers have to stop and scratch their heads to remember any such incidents reported in the postwar era.

Here at Larkspur Farm we observe a minimum distance setback too, because my wife can't stand the smell of chickens. It started out at three hundred feet for the henhouse, six times the Guelph statute, but has since been waived entirely for the meat birds because she finds that pasture-hut chickens don't smell bad at all, as long as you move them every day.

My meat birds are roosters, and for the last two weeks of August they make one hell of a racket, but the neighbours don't complain because they know they're all getting one for Christmas.

Granddaddy's Rules for Country Living

My grandfather, Ira Needles, was the last member of my family to grow up on a working farm. He hated it. He had severe allergies to dust, pollen and animal hair that made the most routine chores unbearable. When he finished high school in 1909, he announced to his father that he was going to go to college so that he could find work off the farm. His father didn't take the news well. He warned my grandfather that if he left, his two brothers would get the farm and he would get nothing. Granddaddy walked out the door and shook the dust (and pollen) of Mount Vernon, Iowa, from his feet.

Fortunately for him, the farm was just twenty miles away from Cedar Rapids, where his uncle and aunt took him in and supported him while he studied business at Coe College, the local institution of higher learning. He took his MBA from Northwestern University in Illinois and went to work for the Goodrich family in Akron, Ohio. In 1926 when the company bought a rubber plant in Kitchener, Ontario, he moved his young family there and rose to become Goodrich Canada's president and chairman in the 1950s.

I think Granddaddy might have been allergic to rubber too. Like a lot of company presidents I have known, he didn't particularly enjoy his life in business. His first love was learning, and he never forgot how that little college in Cedar Rapids had changed his life. He believed every child should have the opportunity to do what he did. In 1956 he took a form of early retirement from Goodrich, organized a circle of friends from the Kitchener business community and announced plans to found what eventually became the University of Waterloo. His second career as the university's chairman of the board of governors and chancellor lasted almost as long as his tenure at Goodrich and gave him far more satisfaction. He finally "retired" at the age of eighty.

I inherited very little of my grandfather's business acumen and all of his allergies. Like him I still spend a good part of the late summer breathing the fumes from a steaming bowl of Vicks-infused water with a towel over my head. But I always admired his courtly manners and quiet authority, and I think, partly to please him, I laboured through four years of economics at the University of Toronto and went to work for an insurance company.

The only time he ever scolded me was when I told him I had bought this little farm. Granddaddy shook his head and said it was "a poor investment" that I would live to regret. He went on to say some other things about my judgment that stung more than a little.

And I said, "Look, just about every one of your eighteen grandchildren is either an artist or a musician. The only one that has attended your precious university has joined the Marxist-Leninists and is now protesting with a placard outside the building they named after you. And I never hear you say anything about his judgment."

Granddaddy chuckled and said, "Chris can stop being a communist anytime he likes. I'm just saying that in my personal experience it's not that easy to get rid of a farm."

We eventually reached a gentlemen's agreement that he would not snipe about my farm as long as I followed his three rules of land ownership: don't buy any machinery; don't keep any livestock; and don't plant any crops.

Granddaddy died at ninety-two, just a couple of years before I left the insurance company, moved to the farm to write plays full-time and raise sheep. Since then I have broken his three rules many times over, and it looks like the ancient cycle is about to be repeated.

Like her great-grandfather, my eldest daughter had no use for farm life and bolted at the first opportunity. Madeline attends the University of Waterloo, where she often finds herself working in the library under the kindly gaze of Granddaddy's portrait. The brass plate on the painting is now tarnished and illegible, and she has decided to have it restored.

She thinks Granddaddy's rules of country property ownership should be inscribed on the plate along with his dates.

Memories of a Country Christmas

There has been a lot of discussion in our house over the last couple of years about the role of "stuff" at Christmas. Like a lot of families across the country, we've been trying to do more with less, and that means looking for meaning somewhere other than in the pile of loot under the tree.

When I ask the children for their favourite memory of Christmas, I find it significant that they seldom recall a particular present. They almost always call up a vision that has been inspired by either ritual or food.

For Heath too Christmas memories are all about visiting, food, music and taking a much-needed break from the relentless demands of a working farm. She loved getting up on a cracking cold Christmas morning and racing out to the barn to feed the animals. She remembers the smell of hot porridge on the wood stove, the drive to the Shelburne nursing home to gather up her grandmother, her adored older brother coming up the lane after a forty-hour drive from the Alberta oilfields. But most of all she remembers the food.

A turkey roasted all day in the kitchen. The table stretched out to accommodate extra people and sagged slightly from the weight of a dozen serving dishes. Every family member had at least one favourite, laced with butter, maple syrup or heavy cream. The rest of the week was given over to visiting, playing instruments and board games.

Our children refer to these memories as Mom's "pioneer stories." But I point out to them that their own memories tend to centre on similar moments and sensations, not presents. Like their mother they remember Christmas Eve drives down to their great-Granny Kate's tiny living room in Creemore, especially the night when Santa himself appeared in the headlights in the falling snow as we passed through the village of Glen Huron. We stopped, and Santa leaned in the car window, called them by name and told them to hurry home to bed. They remember stuffing the sheep and goats with treats in our little barn on Christmas morning and multiple bobsled runs down the treacherous hills at Gramma's farm in the afternoon. And they too remember the food, the music and the visiting.

My own associations with Christmas aren't nearly as intense and aromatic as those of my wife and children. And that isn't just because all of my early Christmases took place in the city. I am descended from a long line of dissenters, free thinkers and party poopers who would tack a single bare wreath on the front door, hand flannel bags of sour candies to one another and go to bed with a book. I do remember, however, as I grew older, carolling in the streets of north Toronto, learning to smoke a pipe with pineapple-flavoured tobacco and drinking tumblers of Grand Marnier. As far as presents go, I tend to recall only the truly wacky ones: a pair of genuine sealskin cufflinks, a satellite tracker (that did nothing of the sort) and a small cardboard box that said "Open Only in Case of Emergency." (Inside it said, "Not Now Stupid—In Case of Emergency!")

Last year the garlands, the ornaments and the nativity scenes all made their usual appearance in our house, but we limited our gift giving to a single item to and from each person. We put up a miniature Christmas tree on a side table in the dining room and opened our presents around it while we ate nectarine puff pancakes with maple syrup.

That was the end of the presents, but it was just the beginning of Christmas.

Free-Range Pig

T his spring, as usual, I loaded an old wooden crate on the back of the truck and drove off to find two young pigs to raise up for the freezer. They go into a pen in the barn for a few weeks until they settle down, and then I let them out in the orchard to fatten over the summer. Meat from pigs raised this way is great—dark and flavourful—and reminds people of what pork used to taste like in the days when pigs lived outside.

The drive gets a little longer every year. The only man I know who still keeps a boar and a few sows lives ten miles away, up over the hill in the wilds of Grey County. This year I decided to bring home an extra pig for my neighbour Hughie, who gave up the last sow herd in this community several years ago. He still misses his pigs, and I thought he needed one to come and visit.

When I got home I backed into the barn, opened the door of the crate, grabbed the first pig by the hind legs and carried him, kicking and screaming, into the pen. Pigs are a lot like teenagers. If something doesn't suit them, they fight and kick and yell their heads off. The second pig went the same way.

The third one looked at me and made one of those instant mental calculations for which pigs are famous. "Wheezy guy with glasses," he said to himself. Then he ducked under my arm, shot off the tailgate, squeezed out under a door and disappeared into the dark.

I slept fitfully that night. The last time this happened to me, I was nine years old. My first two pigs got away through a hole in the pen one night and ran for five miles before they were captured. Pigs can live in the wild indefinitely. They've been domesticated for ten thousand years, but, given the chance, they go feral in about an hour and a half. (Which is another parallel with teenagers, I suppose.) This fugitive had more than a mile of stream and thick bush to hide in and a twenty-acre wheat field to munch on.

"He'll be fine," said my wife. "He'll get lonesome for the others and come back."

"Maybe," I said. "What about coyotes? What if he goes down to the highway?"

The first sighting came the next afternoon, down the road on a neighbour's lawn. But the escapee ducked into the wheat field and headed northwest at a dead run. Hughie's son hopped on his four-wheeler and buzzed around the field to cut him off, but the pig didn't come out. By morning it was on Facebook and had a name: Dillinger.

Hughie came over the next morning. "Don't worry," he said. "Even a pig knows you don't walk away from a place where they're feeding you. Besides, your pig is performing a valuable service. It used to be that you never saw your neighbours all summer unless a pig got out. Pigs do a great job of keeping people in touch."

"You're taking this very well," I said. "He was actually your pig."

The pig went off the radar for three days, and I began to fear the worst. Then I went out to do the chores one evening and stopped short. There was Dillinger, standing in the barn doorway with his head in a tub of feed. I shooed him into the barn, but he flashed the grin of a pig who knows he's at the top of his game, squeezed through a hole in the wall and vanished again.

A few days after that, I was hoeing the garden when Dillinger suddenly came around the henhouse, trotting along like he was on his way to the bank. He was sunburned and covered with dirt. When he heard a "noof" from the pigpen, he paused and sniffed the barn wall. Then he sighed. On a hunch, I walked right past him into the barn and opened the pen door. He hesitated for a moment, looking from the woods to the barn. Then he shrugged, trotted into the pen and flopped down beside his brothers.

Dillinger has shown no interest in going over the wire since then. Some would say he made the fatal mistake of trading a little freedom for a little security. But I don't think he sees it that way. True liberty is the freedom to choose. And Dillinger has opted for three squares a day and freedom of mind.

Year of the Grape

Last winter my son took a sommelier course from the restaurant where he works in the city and came away from it very excited about cultivating grapes and making his own wine. Because the terroir of his student walk-up lies in the shadow of a condo high-rise, it is not particularly favourable to viniculture. He came home one weekend early last spring and asked, "Why don't you plant some grapevines here on the farm, Dad?"

I gave him several reasons. The harsh climate of Nottawasaga Township long ago drove the polar bears north and the rattle-snakes south. It is true that for maybe two weeks in July the place feels like the south of France. Gentle zephyrs waft down over the pastures, caressing the softly lowing cows and gentle sheep. This is when most of the real estate is sold up here.

But for the rest of the year, it is like Nottawasaga Township. The northwest wind gathers speed on the trip from Winnipeg and hurtles over the ice of Georgian Bay, and the first obstacle it smacks into after fifteen hundred miles is our farmhouse.

"That's actually a good thing," said my son. "Grapes like constant air movement. Look at the mistral wind of Provence. The grapes thrive on it."

He had a point. The mistral is *le vent du fada*, the "idiot wind" that blows for weeks at a time, clearing the air of every speck of dust and moisture, and protecting the noble Chardonnay and Cabernet vines from disease. The clarity of the air and the light is what brought the French Impressionist painters to Avignon and Arles. The mistral has inspired much beautiful poetry and has become as important to Provençal culture as food and wine.

A little bit of poetry has been written about our northwesterlies (but because of the excessive use of profanity, none of it has been published). We, too, have our own colony of landscape artists. And because of climate change and new grape varieties, wine production is actually gaining a firm toehold here.

And so I warmed to the idea of grapes. My son outlined his plan, which was fairly simple. He would provide the expertise and I would do the work. He would be the elegant oenologist with book and tasting cup, and I would be the simple, cheerful, ruddy-faced *paysan* with pruning hook and shovel. We visited on the phone every week, discussing varietals that might do well on heavy clay soils that are occasionally buried six feet deep in snow or raided by marauding sheep.

"They say sheep are great at pruning the leaves off the vines and they never eat the fruit," he assured me. I'm not sure about that. Some days my sheep would eat the tires off the truck.

My son inclines toward the refined Cabernets and Chardonnays that grace the linen-covered tables of his restaurant, but our adviser at the Niagara vine nursery explained to us that so far climate change has merely extended the period when vines are exposed to early and late frosts. She predicted we would be skunked every few years if we planted the old European varieties and urged us to pick a hardier vine. I scanned the list and found the Baco Noir.

"This is not one of those aristocratic Old World grapes, which can be fickle and delicate," she explained. "The Baco Noir is a blue-collar grape. It is tough, grows anywhere and will survive extremes of cold and heat. It is vigorous but erratic and sometimes difficult to control."

This is a pretty accurate description of my wife's family, who have been farming these hills for five generations. Baco Noir sounded like a very promising choice.

"But will people drink the stuff?" I asked.

"Oh, of course. The Baco Noir can be very surprising . . . complex, fascinating . . . never predictable."

"That definitely sounds like my wife," I said. "I'm in."

Now that the vines are planted, there is more reading to do on the veranda. My son is studying *Northern Winework: Growing Grapes and Making Wine in Cold Climates*. I just finished *The Worst Pests of the Vineyard*. As I expected, sheep are on the list. So are deer, skunks, raccoons, birds, squirrels, mice, mites, thrips, phylloxera and a host of one-celled fungi.

Eternal vigilance will be the price we pay for a glass of plonk.

A Quack Vet

If you keep animals for food production, you are expected to perform a number of elective medical procedures without professional assistance. Tail docking, deworming, vaccinations, emetics, soporifics, foot treatments, colon irrigations and holistic Shiatsu massage are part of the small farmer's stock-in-trade. We are all genial quacks with well-stocked dispensaries and shelves sagging from the weight of books with titles like *Common Sheep Diseases: Treatment and Cures.* Sheep and chickens have an alarming instinct for self-destruction, especially in the middle of a holiday weekend. The shepherd and poultry man must be on call 24/7 to respond to emergency trauma with either a suture or a shovel.

The natural world is a very violent place. Coyotes roam the fields at night; hawks patrol the skies by day. Livestock must be held in protective custody behind razor wire and high-voltage fences for their own protection. Even so, violence often breaks out within the prison population itself.

I had a trio of hens that did not play well with others. They hived themselves off from the rest of the flock and took up residence on the sheep-pen door. Chickens are cliquey and prickly creatures that are quick to take offence. "Pecking order" is a phrase we use today to describe the unpleasant quality of life in an insurance company or a church group, but it originated from the study of life in the henhouse. Professor Schjelderup-Ebbe, the Norwegian zoologist who coined the phrase, said "defence and aggression in the hen is accomplished with the beak."

The breakaway sect of chickens soon came to blows among themselves on a question of doctrine. Before long, the little grey hen had a bloody patch on the top of her head. So I decided to give the chickens away to a friend who had just purchased one of those elegant mail-order henhouses on wheels and needed a starter flock. I thought maybe a change of scenery would snap them all out of their funk.

At dark I snuck into the sheep barn, snagged the three hens and popped them into a cage overnight. The next morning when I delivered the birds, my friend knelt down to look in the cage and recoiled in horror. "What on earth happened to that chicken?" she cried. I looked more closely and realized the little grey hen hadn't just been pecked . . . she had been scalped . . . by her two closest friends.

What to do? I took the hen home and went to the garden shed for a shovel.

"No, no!" my wife protested. "She's my favourite hen. We can fix her."

My wife is descended from a long line of practical farm people who glance at a suffering chicken, smack it on the head and get on with their day. But that gene somehow skipped her generation. So while she held the hen on the kitchen table, I cleaned it up with antiseptic solution, pulled the flap of skin back up to the crown and put five neat little sutures in her forehead using dental floss. Then we set her down and she walked back to the barn.

That night she settled back on her usual perch alone on the gate of the sheep pen. Apart from the little tufts of dental floss sticking out of her head, she looked pretty good. I gave her a couple of Aspirins and told her to call me in the morning if there was any change.

The next day she came to the veranda for breakfast as usual. When she turned her head, I saw that I had put a little too much tension on one side and her left eyebrow was now pulled up in a pronounced arch that made her look like Gloria Swanson.

Gloria is now eight years old and still lives with the sheep, although this is a poor practice because sheep will pick up a virus from bird droppings if they can't find any other way to do themselves in. But there's something about Gloria that appeals to me. She is a Dissenter, a Party of One, the last member of the True Church. The expression on her face is wary, alert and extremely sceptical about everything, including the medical profession.

When Birds Go Bad

I got into a fight with a rooster last week. I think of myself as a patient person, but it is a waste of time to attempt to reason with a rooster or a ram or a bull. The male animal brain is built the same way as one of those old floppy computer disks with the tab folded over the notch in the right-hand corner. It is designed to carry a certain amount of inherited information but will not accept new information. This is why most roosters, like the one last week, have their heads taken off and go into the pot.

Years ago I had a big showy Dominique rooster that ambushed me one morning. I was minding my own business, prying a rotten fence post out of its hole, when he came at me out of the sun, like a Messerschmitt fighter plane, smacked into the back of my leg and latched on with beak and claws. I yelped and kicked him free, but he ran off and circled back for a second run over the target. By this time I had armed myself with a hoe handle and I caught him with one carefully placed windmill swipe to the back of the head that laid him out in the grass, one foot kicking spasmodically at the air.

I went into the house and told my wife that I had just killed my rooster.

"Oh, dear!" she said. "You liked that rooster. What did you hit him with?"

"A hoe handle," I said.

"Don't worry. You didn't kill him," she assured me. "It takes at least a two-by-four to kill a rooster."

We went back out and, sure enough, the rooster was back on his feet, walking around the orchard. He appeared a little dazed and didn't seem to remember who I was or why he was cross with me. He just shook his head every so often as if he were trying to remember where he put his keys.

Heath told me about a fierce little banty rooster that was her father's pride and joy when she was a little girl. It would attack her whenever she came out to the barn, and she hated it. But her father loved that bird. One day she was helping him with the pump and he told her to run up to the barn and turn on the tap in the stable. She was wearing shorts and she knew the rooster would be somewhere in the barn, so she picked up a two-by-four and crept into the dark stable as quietly as she could. The rooster came out of nowhere, but this time she was ready for him. She nailed him squarely with a two-base hit that sent the bird the length of the hallway and into the gutter for the stable cleaner. Then she was overcome with remorse.

"I've killed my dad's favourite rooster," she wailed. "He'll be so upset." She went to the tap to turn on the water, wondering how she was going to break the news to him. She came back and bent over to look at the bird. He looked as dead as a doornail, completely stiff with his feathers fluffed out. She prodded him carefully with the board and he slowly opened one eye.

"Oh my!" I said. "What did you do?"

"I hit him again."

But the banty rooster survived. He lived on the windowsill of the stable for a couple of years until one night a big wind came along, sucked the window and the rooster out of the wall and took them both back to the bush. Only the window was found.

"So I'd get a two-by-four if I were you," she said. "And don't leave that post hole the way it is. Somebody's bound to step in it."

After lunch I was carrying two pails of water to the hens when I felt hot claws sink into my upper thigh. I danced three steps to the left and went up to my hip in the post hole. The pails of water followed. Back at the house, I reported that I had filled in the post hole.

"That was quick," said Heath.

"Yes," I said. "The rooster died suddenly and I used that hole to bury him."

A Blast from the Past

C anada is a land of committees. Years ago, there was a joke making the rounds that every country had its own distinct form of social organization. If three or more countrymen got together, in Italy they would instantly become a political party, in France they would start a union, and in Britain they would form a queue. Here in Canada they would organize a panel discussion.

I have served on enough committees to know that we do have a habit of jawing a thing to death before we pick up a shovel, but our history tells us we also respect a firm voice and a clear call to action.

For example, there was an old fieldstone church that once stood on the Little farm on the 7th Line of Mulmur Township, just north of Highway 89. The cemetery attached to Old St. Luke's is still maintained today, although the church itself has been gone for nearly ninety years. The cluster of gravestones in the shade of ancient maple trees carries the names of Littles, McNabbs, Gallaughers and many other families from the first days of the township.

I gave a little talk to a neighbourhood audience a few years ago and mentioned how, as a boy, I often rode horseback past the remains of the old church, which had burned to the ground in

1926. During the reception afterwards, Lucille Burley, an elderly woman who had been born on the Little farm, came over to correct me. This often happens when I make any observation about the past in Rosemont.

"Did I get the date wrong about the fire?" I asked.

"The date was probably right. But it didn't burn down."

"What happened to it then?"

"They blew it up."

"Really?" I said. "Nobody ever told me anything about it blowing up."

"I don't think many people know what really happened. I only know from a few things my father told me. But it's so long ago, it's probably safe to tell the story now."

The old church stood on a lot the family had donated in 1860, but by the 1920s it had fallen into disrepair and the elders were reluctant to pour more money into it. The congregation wrangled over the problem for ten years while the roof leaked and wind whistled through the cracks in the stone walls. Eventually a portion of the congregation broke away and began construction of a new brick church a mile away in the village of Rosemont, proposing to christen it St. Luke's as well.

Faced with the prospect of a permanent rift in the church family, one of the wardens went over to the old church in broad daylight and placed a charge of dynamite in the basement. The explosion levelled the building and left the Anglicans with no choice but to gather in the new St. Luke's. This is the same church my wife and I were married in.

"Do they have any idea who the guy was that placed the dynamite?" I asked.

"Oh, yes," she said. "It was John McNabb."

"But one of the stained-glass windows above the altar is dedicated to a John McNabb. Would that be the same man?"

She nodded. "People were ever so grateful to John. Without him, the split in the church might have lasted for decades. It was a very painful subject for a lot of people for many years, and families were careful not to speak about it. My father certainly never got over it. But it's all forgotten now."

The three stained-glass windows show a scene of Jesus with a flock of sheep. The inscription below reads, "Feed My Sheep." As a shepherd myself, I know that sheep are not easily led. This helps to explain why they turn up so often in Scripture. Sheep were first domesticated six thousand years ago and have been hybridized to the point that they are a completely human-made animal, the work-in-progress of a committee that has been meeting on the third Thursday of the month since the early Bronze Age.

Canadians are certainly not sheep. We are talkers because we prefer to move forward as a group. But we are also a fractious and disputatious tribe that sometimes needs a rugged individualist to bring closure to a discussion and cast a "weighted" vote. In the end we understand that the group is more important than any building. And, to draw from another corner of the barnyard, you can't make an omelette without breaking a few eggs.

The Postman

O ne of the neighbours died last winter, and we didn't hear the news for nearly three weeks. This never would have happened in the days when Kenny Jardine kept us up to date.

Kenny lived across the Ninth Concession from us at the end of a long lane in a little white house hidden by willow trees. I met him in the spring of 1978, just after I had taken possession of the property, and he told me all about the abandoned farmhouse I planned to restore.

"You know it's haunted," he said. Then he told me about a woman who contracted rabies and jumped out the upstairs window. This was the sort of story he loved, because it required expanding a thing to proportions that satisfied his imagination.

Kenny's observations often found their way into my "fables," as he used to call them. It's a good word, fables. I've never found a better one to describe my writing. I've lost count of the ideas he gave me, sitting in his kitchen beside the wood stove or leaning on the box of the pickup truck at the mailbox. Like me, he was vague about dates and always looked for colour and dialogue that brought a story to life.

One time we were standing out at the mailbox in a howling wind off the lake, and Kenny reported that one of the neighbours had driven south to Orlando to escape the winter and died there the week before Christmas.

"Terrible time to die in Florida," he said. And after a pause he added, "Pretty good time to die up here."

The party line I shared with Kenny was the forerunner to the internet chat room and essential for staying abreast of current affairs. Every morning I would log on with Kenny and his friend Helen Kenwell, who lived up in Maxwell, to listen to the news and their comments. They covered the hard news first—births, deaths, break-ins—and then moved to items of human interest, for example, the police had mistaken deer guts in the ditch for a murder. Once he was loaded with all the current events, he would set off like a postman to spread the word. He had a milk and cookies route that took him across the fields to the kitchens of the Jardine Sideroad and the Blind Line. I have several photographs of him, but the image that sticks in my mind is a bent figure moving across the field, tilted slightly forward, his legs moving quickly, almost in a trot and eating up the miles like a coyote.

If we knew each other well as neighbours in those days, it was because Kenny laid down the fibre optic cables between our houses. He pollinated from flower to flower, checked to see that smoke was coming out of the chimney. He remembered birthdays and anniversaries, reflected over a hot biscuit, patted the dog and moved on.

Because he walked everywhere and didn't carry an ounce of fat, Kenny enjoyed basically good health for eighty-four years. When he finally made the trip to the hospital and received the diagnosis of a terminal illness, the doctors worried about the possibility he had picked up some superbug and put him in isolation. Cutting Kenny off from human contact was about the best way to torture him. I had to don a gown, mask and gloves to get in to see him, and when I finally opened the door, he said, "Huloo! Did you hear they saw a moose on the Min Baker Sideroad yesterday?" I had not heard that. This was breaking news, and I must have looked astonished. "I still have the phone," he shrugged.

He returned to the hospital after Christmas and went down quickly. I watched the room fill up every night with his extended family—an extraordinary thing for a man who lived alone for much of his life. When Kenny was past the point of talking, the visiting went on around his bedside until the nurses eased us all out and we stood yakking in the parking lot. It was a shame Kenny couldn't join in, because it was the kind of evening he loved best.

E.B. White once said that as a writer he felt charged with the safekeeping of all items of worldly or unworldly significance, as if he would be held personally accountable if any of them were to be lost. Kenny knew I felt the same way and fed my habit.

The Information Age of Instant Everything has overtaken Kenny and his like. Now that I am reduced to *The Globe and Mail* and Twitter, I feel dangerously underinformed.

A Puff of Straw

On a cold night last November, I was climbing a ladder in the barn to get some hay bales down for the sheep, the same ladder I have climbed daily for over twenty-five years. I stepped over onto the haymow floor and put my foot on a puff of straw that went out from under my boot like a bar of soap. Next thing I knew I was hanging by my fingers from the edge of the haymow. But fingers do not support me anymore, and I dropped six feet down onto the arms of the loader tractor, bounced once and landed full length in the manure bucket.

This was not good. My right leg and my left arm wouldn't work, and breathing was very painful. I have never carried a cell phone around the farm and had no way to signal the house. My trusty guard dog Dexter was sleeping on the chesterfield in front of the fire, dreaming of rabbits. I tried to pull myself up into a sitting position with my writing hand, which has never failed me yet, but the most I could manage was to slither out of the bucket like an inchworm and get my head up against the front tire of the tractor. There was nothing else to do but lie there patiently and wait until my wife noticed I was missing. She would probably send my daughter out to look for me first, so it was important not to alarm her too much. I tried to keep my head up and began practising an opening line.

"I've had a little mishap here."

Irony is lost on sheep. They studied me through the steel gate of their pen, puzzled as always by my behaviour. "Why is he lying on the floor talking to himself when we need a bale of hay?"

The temperature had dipped to the freezing mark and a stiff wind blew across the concrete floor. I was wearing a heavy barn coat, but my legs were stretched out into that wretched wind. Within minutes I began to shiver.

Whenever I am in pain, facing extensive dental work or sitting through an evening of throat singing and interpretive dance, I close my eyes and go to a special place I call "airport mode." The last time I whacked myself this severely was about twenty years ago, falling out of the same haymow and landing in the same place. On that occasion I had an excuse, because I was escaping from a nest of angry yellow jackets. I didn't get stung, but I did crush my heel and ever since have limped on rainy days, the way all my wife's brothers and western cousins limp. Not quite the same, for they are cowboys, and a cowboy's limp is part of his rugged charm. When a writer limps, people just assume it is stiffness brought on by too much deskwork. I tried telling people that my bull-riding days were over, but no one took me seriously.

The sheep gave up and lay down without their supper. The wind howled and the barn doors banged. My neighbour drove by in his truck, but he was scanning the road for my dog and not looking at the barn. I drifted in and out of consciousness and lost track of time.

Then suddenly she was there in the doorway carrying a barn lantern, my very own Florence Nightingale. The dog was beside her, very sheepish that he had been dozing instead of dashing to the house to write "Fire" in the mashed potatoes. No citation for bravery for Dexter.

"I've had a little mishap here," I said, teeth chattering uncontrollably.

Farm women always curse their husbands for two minutes before they call an ambulance. That's because they saw this coming and can't understand why you would own a ladder and not learn to tie it off. Then she put a blanket over me and held my hand.

Some people sit on a waiting list for a year for a hip replacement. If you fling yourself off a cliff, the doctors will do it the next morning, but I don't recommend it. Thanks to the miracle of modern medicine, I am walking again without a cane, not quite sure which leg to limp on.

The Green Philosopher

A few years ago my son called from university in Halifax, where he was wading through the nihilist philosophers in a very determined search for the meaning of life.

"So what are you up to?" he asked.

"Cleaning out my henhouse," I replied.

"You're always cleaning out the henhouse, Dad. You know, Nietzsche said that there are a finite number of things in the universe and an infinite amount of time, and that explains why the same stuff happens over and over again."

"Thanks for clearing that up," I said. "Are you enjoying Mr. Nietzsche?"

"I guess so. I'm not sure that you're supposed to enjoy reading someone who says that God is dead, nature has no moral foundation and life is meaningless. Actually, they have a big problem down here because a lot of kids get depressed after they take this course."

"I can't imagine why. How are you handling it?"

"Okay, I guess. I think the trick is to just open yourself to the sublime indifference of the universe."

When I was my son's age, I too spent a lot of time figuring out life, leaning on a couple of Stoic philosophers for a while as I made my way through school and into the city's corridors of power. But when life's great questions loomed too large, I always found that a trip back to the old farm community where I was raised never failed to lift my spirits. I loved the rhythm of the fieldwork and the wonderful voices that came out of that neighbourhood. For a long time I thought it was the dreamy romantic in me that sent me back to those country roads, trying to recapture a lost world. But as I have grown older, with my own little farm and family, I have come to a clearer understanding of what drew me to this way of life.

What I admired most about the farmers I knew as a young man was the way they got out of bed in the morning and started looking after the life around them. That's what a farmer was supposed to do. When you take responsibility for the life around you, it gives you a sense of purpose and makes you feel important. Not the kind of importance that comes from seeing your picture in the newspaper after you've picked up a prestigious award. It's the feeling that comes from knowing that living things depend on you. As an old farmer in Mono Township once said to me, "Danny, even a chicken can be glad to see you." This helps to explain why so many of those old guys carried on long after any financial incentive had disappeared and their accountant was begging them to give it up. Because it still felt like the right thing to be doing. They took pleasure in a pen of fat lambs, a stand of corn or the progress of a boy learning to scuffle that corn.

I like looking after stuff too. This is the only explanation I can offer for keeping a small flock of sheep and trying to farm like the year was 1955. The sheep are always happy to see me, and they make me feel important.

I'm not conspicuously green or organic, but I do listen attentively to the pantheon of food-producing deities in the world today, from the herbalist on the left to the herbicidal on the right, and I pick up all sorts of nifty tricks to apply in the garden and the pastures. I try to step lightly on the earth. And as proof that this approach works, I will show you two sleek, seventeen-year-old barn cats, for no creature wears the scratches and dents of a high-impact lifestyle more visibly than a barn cat.

Nietzsche's nihilism did him no good in the end. He was ignored for much of his career and eventually expired in an asylum. His last conversation in the outside world was with a horse. I always thought poor Fred lived inside his head too much and would have been better off if he kept a few sheep. He might have liked them, and liking is always a comfort in a cold world. As another great philosopher, the poet Wendell Berry, once wrote, we are "joined to each other and the whole joined to nature, to the world, by liking, by delighted and affectionate understanding."